BY EDDIE HUANG

Fresh Off the Boat

Double Cup Love

DOUBLE CUP LOVE

SPIEGEL & GRAU

NEW YORK

DOUBLE CUP LOVE

ON
THE TRAIL
OF
FAMILY, FOOD,
AND
BROKEN
HEARTS IN
CHINA

EDDIE HUANG

Published in the United States by Spiegel & Grau,
an imprint of Random House,
a division of Penguin Random House LLC, New York.

SPIEGEL & GRAU and the HOUSE colophon are
registered trademarks of Penguin Random House LLC.

LIBRARY OF CONGRESS CATALOGING-IN-PUBLICATION DATA
Names: Huang, Eddie
Title: Double cup love : on the trail of family, food,
and broken hearts in China / Eddie Huang.
Description: New York : Spiegel & Grau, 2016.
Identifiers: LCCN 2015029722| ISBN 9780812995466
(hardback : acid-free paper) | ISBN 9780812995473 (ebook)
Subjects: LCSH: Huang, Eddie, 1982—Travel—China. | Taiwanese Americans—Travel—China. | Cooking—China. | Food trucks—China. | Taiwanese Americans—Ethnic identity. | Taiwanese Americans—Biography. | Huang, Eddie, 1982—Family. | Huang, Eddie, 1982—Relations with women. | Marriage—Social aspects—United States. | Love—Social aspects—United States. | BISAC: BIOGRAPHY & AUTOBIOGRAPHY / Cultural Heritage. | SOCIAL SCIENCE / Customs & Traditions.
Classification: LCC E184.T35 H83 2016 | DDC 647.95092—dc23
LC record available at http://lccn.loc.gov/2015029722

Printed in the United States of America on acid-free paper

randomhousebooks.com
spiegelandgrau.com

246897531

First Edition

Book design by Barbara M. Bachman

Thanks, Mom & Dad

TELESCOPES,
BINOCULARS,
THE FEDS HATE
MY VERNACULAR.

— CAM'RON

THE CRIB SCARFACE
COULDN'T BE MORE TONY.
YOU LOVE ME FOR ME
COULD YOU BE MORE PHONY?

— KANYE

NOW TAKE THESE WORDS HOME
AND THINK IT THROUGH
OR THE NEXT RHYME I WRITE
MIGHT BE ABOUT YOU.

— PRODIGY

PROLOGUE

I arrived at the end of my vision only to realize it was another door to confusion: "dun-dun-dun-bana-nana-nana-na-na-naaa-naaa."*

I could hear Bird in my head and it was starting to make sense.

Like "Parker's Mood" jumping out in a moment of satori, I took my cue from the horns and put my head down, sprinting toward the finish. I stumbled over the keys, tried to understand the drums, but really just improvised my way to the end, where I realized that all that was waiting for me was another epiphany, the same one that started it all three minutes and eight seconds earlier: "dun-dun-dun-bana-nana-nana-na-na-naaa-naaa." But unlike the first time I heard Parker's sax, this realization wasn't hope in the face of rejection. It was despair in the face of acceptance. That old, harrowing, reluctant motherfucker despair staring you in the face with empty hands upturned: "dun-dun-dun-bana-nana-nana-na-na-naaa-naaa."

You listen to his loop at the beginning of the song thinking that by the end you'll be all brand-new, but nothing. It gives you hope with a faint whisper through reeds, takes you on an impromptu journey to nowhere, and drops you right back off where you started with the same loop and a double dose of despair echoing over and over "dun-dun-dun-bana-nana-nana-na-na-naaa-naaa."

This was the sound in my head as I watched Kevin Spacey delivering a monologue in *House of Cards*:

---

* That's the sax at the beginning of Charlie Parker's "Parker's Mood."

There are two kinds of pain. The sort of pain that makes you strong or useless pain. The sort of pain that's only suffering. I have no patience for useless things.

Was it useless, though? Before I could figure it out, I felt my heart stop, my face turn gray, and my body disconnect from my mind. I sat there on the couch at my friend Gary's house in Houston, right across the street from the Galleria. And I realized I was dying.

I couldn't breathe, scared that the last thing I'd ever feel on this earth before I became fish food was Kevin Spacey's politico-sexual-predator vibes. My face got stuck as I fell off the couch onto the floor underneath the coffee table, where Gary's AR-15 rested.

How is it legal for Gary to watch Celtic games with an AR-15 around his neck? How is it legal for anyone to walk into a Walmart and cop a six-inch Subway meatball sub, an AR-15, and the "Everything Is Awesome" single in the same shopping cart? Something's got to give.

It was my body.

It didn't make sense. This wasn't supposed to happen. I'd just gotten my shit straight. I had my bills on autopay! I had to get to Evan. When everyone else in the family left me, there was always Evan. Emery was my ace, Mom was my heart, Dad was the judge, but Evan was my caretaker. I crawled slowly and deliberately. It took every neuron in my brain to communicate with my legs. It was as if rigor mortis had already set in, flesh stiff like upper lips. I had to fight.

I couldn't stand, so I kept grabbing at the ground and pulling myself forward with the little traction I could create against the floor. To the reasonable woman or man reading this, you have to understand that my body was gelatinous, I had achieved perfect rehydrated sea cucumber status* and for the second time in my life, it occurred to me that my

---

* My mom always loved sea cucumber, and the technique she was most proud of was her ability to re-hydrate dried sea cucumber perfectly.

mother would be proud, a thought that kept me going as I pushed my body along by pressing my feet against the moldings at the bottom of the wall. Eventually, I got to the door of Evan's room.

I could see Evan! I might not be dead! I grabbed the side of the door and pulled myself up with the last bit of energy I had.

"EVAN! HELP!"

He rolled over in his bed to look at me, unimpressed.

"Dude, what are you doing? You look like a psycho leaning against the door like that."

"EVAN . . . I just died."

"What?"

"I just died, man. For real, my spirit left my body."

"Your what? Left your what?"

"MY SPIRIT LEFT MY BODY! I DIED!"

Evan realized this wasn't the garden-variety late-night self-realization. He jumped to his feet and stared me in the eyes.

"EDDIE! What did you do? Your eyes are yellow!"

"I ate the indica hash beef jerky!"

"So did I! So did Gary! Stop being a bitch."

"I ate all of it. . . ."

"ALL OF IT?"

"And some of the weed cupcake."

He slapped me.

"Wake the fuck up! You didn't die. What's wrong, man?"

"My heart stopped. My face got stuck. I felt like gelatin and then everything went gray."

All the noise woke Gary up from his nap.

"What are you guys doing?"

"I'm dying."

"BAHAHAHAHAHA, how are you dying standing in the doorway, you stupid fuck?"

"It's gone, Gary. My essence is gone. I'm never going to be the same. The Matrix accepted me."

"Oh my god, do we have to take this fool to the hospital?"

"Calm down. This happened to him before."

"When?"

"Two years ago, on Orchard Street. We were broke living in an apartment: me, Emery, Eddie, and Ning"—my ex-girlfriend—"on three mattresses side by side. There was only about six hundred dollars left in the Baohaus"—my restaurant in the East Village—"account, and Eddie used two hundred to buy an air conditioner 'cause it was hot. Eddie got really high, Emery got really mad, tried to fight Eddie, and Eddie didn't want to fight Emery so he ran around the apartment complex with no clothes on, screaming, 'What do you want from me? Take everything!'"

"You think he's gonna start running around my apartment with no clothes on?"

"No one should run around your apartment, Gary, there are two AR-15s in the living room!" I managed to yell.

"Eddie, if you fucking mention gun control again, I'm gonna kick you out of my house."

"NO! NO! NO, GARY! I will not shut up! I have to speak up. I have to keep fighting because the day you stop fighting is the day you die!"

I could feel my legs, and my cheeks tingled. The front of my forehead still felt stiff and numb, but I was suddenly hungry.

"EAT! I have to eat!"

I ran to Gary's kitchen and grabbed the first thing I saw in the pantry: Cheez-Its. Took the box, opened it up, and poured Cheez-Its into my mouth hoping that I could feel them.

"I'm alive! I'm alive! I can chew! I can eat! I'm not dead!"

"OK, I think we might need to take him to the hospital, something's really wrong," said Evan.

"Something is DEFINITELY wrong, he's dancing on fucking Cheez-Its in my kitchen, dude!"

I wanted to make sure I was alive, so I'd poured Cheez-Its on the floor and started stepping on them one by one.

"Intention! You see that, Gary? Life is about intentions. I am man; I intend to step on this Cheez-It!"

———

We packed into Gary's car and drove to the hospital, where I did jumping jacks for fifteen minutes while I waited to see the doctor.

"What is that boy doing?" asked the receptionist.

"I'm staying alive!"

"Boy, you ain't at the disco, so you better sit your ass down."

"I can't, ma'am. I'm sorry, but the day you don't want to be alive, your spirit will leave you."

"Eddie, sit the fuck down," said Evan.

"No! I'm not trying to cause any trouble, but you have to fight to stay alive, ma'am. Every day, you have to fight. If you accept the world or let it accept you, you'll be erased. I mean, you can accept it if that's a conscious acceptance, but it has to be intended. Life is about intention."

She stood up behind the counter.

"Boy, I don't know what kind of drugs you did, but you need to sit DOWN because you freakin' everybody out."

"It was the beef jerky, ma'am."

"This boy overdosed on beef jerky?"

"It was marijuana beef jerky, ma'am."

"Marijuana? Please . . . let me go get a doctor. I can't have this man doing jumping jacks in my waiting room."

Five minutes later, I was admitted into a room where a nurse checked my vitals.

"You need to be still while I do this, sir."

"OK, I will sit, but I want you to know I'm alive."

"Yes, sir, you are alive but your blood pressure is low."

"I died about forty-five minutes ago."

The nurse looked at me quizzically and wrote on a clipboard.

"The doctor will be in to see you."

As I waited, I started doing squats using my own body weight, flexing my lower leg muscles to make sure they were still firing. After about ten minutes, the doctor finally arrived. He was a tall white man, with glasses. Nothing else really stuck out about him.

"So you ate some marijuana beef jerky?"

"Yes, sir, yes, I did, and then I died."

"I heard you were doing jumping jacks, I see you doing squats now, the nurse took your vitals, and besides a little low blood pressure, everything is fine."

"Sir, I agree that I may be OK now, but about forty-five minutes ago I died."

"Son, there is nothing I can do for you medically, but man to man, if you're going to eat weed I have a bit of advice for you."

"What is that, sir?"

"Don't be such a pussy about it."

"I'll try, but I'm starting to think that this is all there is."

"What's all there is?"

"Being a pussy."*

"Come again?"

"Running. I gotta keep running."

---

* He said it first! I assure you I would never use pussy as a pejorative.

PART 1

LOVE

Connie

When it all came crashing down in Houston, I was dating Connie. I met her on OKCupid, but she claimed she'd seen me on the train before, and in some metaphysical way, I felt like I already knew her, too. She was Chinatown ice cream, a seeming contradiction considering that most Chinatown residents shart their pants when introduced to lactose. Ice cream was a foreign object our bodies rejected, but being raised in America, we wouldn't be denied. We wanted our gummy bears. We wanted our hamburgers. We wanted our fucking ice cream.

In the Chinatown ice cream truck there was always red bean, green tea, and the dreaded durian, but Connie represented a special flavor that anyone from Rowland Heights to Fairfax, Virginia, would recognize: black sesame. Our parents put red bean in ice cream, and Japanese heads even had matcha, but the greatest contribution my generation of Asian Americans has made to ice cream is undoubtedly black sesame. We'd seen black sesame in tong yuan, fried sesame balls, and even pancakes, but to infuse creamy, whole-milk, lactose-laden ice cream with black sesame was extremely fucking future. Each generation must have its own ice cream. This was ours.

We complain about silenced minorities and the lack of Asian-American voices in our culture, but it's not that we don't talk. Go to any boba spot or Chinatown ice cream shop on a Friday night, and you'll hear a lot of chicken talk. If you happen to be reading this book in Alabama, and there isn't a Chinatown ice cream shop for you to peep game, just go on Yelp,* which is also Exhibits A, B, and C for the squawking Chinese American. Nothing encapsulates the over-reduced Chinese-American mind better than Yelp. We aren't quiet, we aren't devoid of opinion—we're an extremely passive-aggressive, tribal, prescriptive people who can't agree on how we feel about Indians. But it's extremely East Asian to even ask these questions, i.e., how should we feel about Indians as a group, as a race, but not as individuals? Other Asians—like Filipinos—are much better about these things and much more liberal in their acceptance and understanding of life in general, but if we keep it to the Dogmatic Three—China, Korea, and Japan—every opinion was reductive and authoritarian.

In Korea you have chaebols,† in China you have Confucianism-Maoism-Momism, while Japan has legislation on the proper way to fold and present a receipt. I once walked into a 7-11 in Tokyo, got a Pocari Sweat, took a sip of said Pocari Sweat, then walked up to the register to pay. When I reached the counter, homie said to me: "You should not do that in Japan."

"Do what?"

"Drink the Pocari Sweat before you pay."

"Is this rule specific to Pocari Sweat?"

"No, anything. Do not eat or drink before you pay."

"Are you from America? 'Cause your English doesn't sound like you grew up in Japan."

"I am *definitely* Japanese. I was born in Japan, then went to high school in California and came back to Japan so I know how people in America drink things before they pay, but you should not do it in Japan. It is very offensive."

"But I'm paying."

"It doesn't matter, I already thought bad things about you."

"Like what?"

---

* yelp.com/biz/chinatown-ice-cream-factory-new-york.

† Five or six conglomerates control almost all business in South Korea. Most people are born and raised with the end goal of working for one of these chaebols.

"That you are a thief."

"What if I don't care what you think?"

"This is very dishonorable."

It occurred to me early on that as an Asian American what I think about myself doesn't really matter, nor do intentions, because the ultimate arbiter of our lives is public opinion. We go through our lives making calculations based on expectations and declaring judgments using our advanced research skills despite never really touching, seeing, or feeling the things we're judging. While the West anchors identity in the autonomous mind—"I think, therefore I am"—Asian identity is the sum of our judgments of other people: "I side-eye, therefore I am."

Connie was an avatar of Generation Black Sesame but chose to quarantine herself in the old Asian-American mold. On our first date, she told me she had moved to N.Y. from L.A. largely because she read my blog, loved food, and related to everything I said about Asian identity—the power of an ancient culture hurtling forward unbound from arbitrary restraints—but I doubted it. She had been formulating all types of ideas for Baohaus from California; she criticized our forays into vegetarian curry, and seemingly had a plan for my life before ever meeting me. My mom was the same. I'm pretty sure the minute my dad's Calpico hit the lips of her vagina, she was screaming: "I understand you!" "I know what you need!" "You must keep bar license active!"*

Connie was a less effective American remake of my mom cloaked in skin-tight racerback dresses. If you told Connie and my mom to get to the same 99 Ranch Market from the same starting point, my mom would get there twenty minutes faster, taking back streets and residential service roads, while Connie would sit on the 405 driving in the sand,† arriving at the 99 Ranch Market after all the good hollow heart vegetable was already bought up.

---

* I once got a zero-star review from Sam Sifton at *The New York Times,* and my mom's response was "You must keep bar license active!"

† Shangri-Las, "Walking in the Sand"—best cut from *Goodfellas.*

I'd seen girls like her at Taiwanese-Chinese gatherings for years. My aunts and uncles loved propping them up.

"She has straight A's! So smart."

"You must see her play violin, great form, beautiful hands, how you say . . . exaquisite! Yes, exaquisite!"

"Her face very generous will bring luck to a family."

My cousin Wendy was like this. She went to Yale, was relatively tall, had the titty buffet on smash, and got paraded around at all our events in some derivative of the qipao. It was like she won the Heisman every weekend and did the potluck circuit for her adoring fans. The only thing she didn't have was bound feet. That would have unified all the belts in her weight class.

Taiwanese-Chinese people just assume we all see the same math so there's no hesitation when pouring on the compliments. Nor do parents hesitate in pointing out your girl's bad fortune. For years, I heard complaints about my ex.

"Eddie's girlfriend, Vivienne,* has stingy face. Bad fortune, she will take all your luck."

"Limp, too! Bad energy. I saw her wipe the table! She doesn't clean, she just smears the sauce into table more. Who taught her to wipe a table?"

"Eyes are small. Not generous. That's why she doesn't want to clean."

ALL OUR EYES ARE SMALL, WHAT ARE YOU AUNTS AND UNCLES TALKING ABOUT?

Connie was the first woman I ever dated that could have been potluck-approved. For that reason, I stayed in the relationship, because hate-smashing the superficial ideals your race has held over your head is victory between the sheets. She knew kung fu, she had won an East L.A. beauty contest, and her father was a herbal medicinist, but it all felt extremely foreign to me. Not only did she not understand my Dipset references, but all she wanted to talk about was vegetables and being Asian. It was as if her entire life revolved around race and vegetarianism, which

---

* Real name changed to the most popular Taiwanese name for women.

after a while start to feel like the same thing. When all else fails in romance, do people just give up and marry the manifestation of their favorite restaurant? I guess that would explain why so many people in middle America look like they married a Cheesecake Factory.

But I couldn't resist. The relationship started off like the *Spring Breakers* experience* got white glove–delivered to my couch: kung fu grip on the throat, lobster sauce on the walls, Gucci Mane might as well have been watching in a bathtub. She was fresh out of culinary school, working at Shady Roots, and would come over right after her prep shift in the afternoon 'cause she liked riding reverse while *Yo! MTV Raps* was on. It was around the time "Rack City"—Tyga's strip-club anthem—came out, which made me want to throw change around my living room 'cause I'm too chcap to throw Washingtons at someone who's already agreed to have sex with me. Like George Bush paintings or French Montana records, it was extremely entertaining but devoid of any deeper enrichment.

She was the Carl Lewis of my single life. In record time (thirteen days), she started leaving all her things in my crib, stayed over every night, woke me up at random hours to tell me about sweet potato muffins and ask if I was listening to her. I didn't realize what was going on until it was too late.

"You know, Serena's recipes are so smart. We're making sweet potato muffins at work."

"Dope," I mumbled.

"It's one of those recipes where it's not just a substitute muffin that isn't as good as the non-vegan ones, it's actually so much better."

"That's awesome. Nobody wants to be Plan B, not even a sweet potato muffin."

"Yeah, it really bothers me when people assume vegan food can't be as tasty. It's not less delicious because it's vegan. I think it's actually better."

---

* Most beautiful and ignorant thing I've seen in years was James Franco as Alien in *Spring Breakers*.

"Vegan discrimination is super fucked up."

"Are you making fun of me?"

"No, I definitely agree that vegan food shouldn't be discriminated against, and I'm ready to march."

"You don't have to listen to me if you don't want to."

"You gotta let me live. It's two A.M. on a Tuesday and you're talking to me about vegan food discrimination and sweet potato muffins. Do you think anyone in the universe wants to talk about this right now?"

"Why are you so mean?"

"I'm not mean, I'm just not interested. You need to talk to someone else about the plight of vegan food identity politics."

"What is wrong with you? You are so crazy!"

"And I really think a lot of people would agree with you. I'll even agree with you if I can go to sleep."

"If you don't want me to be here, you can just tell me."

In all honesty, I wished she didn't stay over. The sex was face-melting, but I hated feeling like I was staring the rest of my life in its muffin afterward. I lied to her anyway.

"I want you to be here."

There was nothing wrong with Connie. My boy David kept saying "she checks a lot of boxes," and he was right. Connie came into my life, rearranged my kitchen, cleaned my room, befriended Evan, got me eating breakfast, and kept the crib smellin' like lotion. But it only made me even more suspicious. What did she want? She was definitely trying to trap me, but why me? Why did I deserve this?

And why did she double-plate breakfast?*

My room doesn't even have a door, but my plate got a plate, the eggs had miso, and the salad had microgreens. The food was delicious, the service was incredible, but I was uncomfortable. Everything Connie did made me feel like I was an orphan being relocated to the Russian Tea

---

* She would bring the plate out on top of another plate like some fine dining shit.

Room, but I liked my lo-fi lo-life. Evan appreciated Connie more than I did.

"It's nice having Connie around."

"It's O.D."

"Son, this apartment was Iraq before she came."

"Iraq has its charms. And people in Iraq don't want to eat kebabs on two plates."

"Ha ha, yo, why do you care if she uses two plates? She washes them anyway."

"It just doesn't make sense! We're in a shit apartment, why is she trying to make it Le Bernardin?"

"She got plans for herself, my g."

"That's what I'm sayin'! She got plans for me and I can tell they're really bad plans. They're like Dad's plans when his friends came over to the house!"

"Fuck, I hated those plans."

"I'm saying!"

"All right, family, everybody wake up! Wake up, Huang family! Let's do some cleaning today!" my dad would scream over our home intercom system.

"Shut the fuck up! I'm sleeping, you dick," screamed Emery.

"That's no way to talk to your father! Let's do some cleaning, boys!"

When my dad used his Cattleman's Steakhouse* country western voice, you knew he wanted something. Maybe he wanted his laser discs dusted? His car washed? Or maybe just someone to pick up balls at the tennis court while he practiced slice serving, but most of the time when he used the intercom system in the morning he was having friends over.

"Nobody help clean! Who cares about his stupid friends?" screamed my mom.

---

* Cattleman's was my pops's restaurant, an Orlando steakhouse.

My mom was willing to clean our messes up,* but the buck stopped with outsiders. Whatever the family needed, she was willing, but being the family's maid was enough. She refused to clean for anyone else.

And even when she was straightening up the house, Pops never made it easy. While my mother was cleaning, my father was always creating more shit to clean. If my mom was doing laundry and picking up dirty clothes, son would walk past her and throw his shirt on the floor or leave a trail of dirty socks from the door into the bedroom. He'd ignore her standing there with a laundry bag in her hand and justified it in his mind because he paid the bills. I remember he once said to my mom, "I didn't get married to wash my own shirt."

Usually I enjoyed my dad's Al Bundy schtick, but that wasn't right. I promised myself that one day I'd meet a woman with her own money and career so we could go half on a white male college dropout to wash our shirts and dust our laser discs.

"You are a pig! So dirty all the time, why don't you show your friends how dirty you are!" screamed my mom.

"I dare you to say that to me again," my dad said, ice dripping from his voice.

I always wished my mom would leave it at that and just let us do the cleaning, but she couldn't let it go.

"You aren't shit! All you care about is friends! Oh, look at me, Louis Huang, so successful, come to my house, eat my food, make a mess, sing karaoke, and let my wife do all the cleaning!"

"I got you a maid!"

"There are five people, three dogs, thirty friends coming over, and you let me get *one* maid. What math is this? Too funny, Shoo Sin!† Too funny!"

And then they'd fight. She'd do something like throw boiling water at

---

* For the record, Evan and I always helped clean. Emery seldom helped clean, but he did spend a lot of time arguing with my dad so we credit him as a lobbyist for labor.

† My dad's Chinese name.

him. Tell him he wasn't a man and then he'd grab her by the hair, smack her around, drag her across the floor, and everything got broken. Plates, glasses, our fucking humanity, everything was destroyed for his cot damn friends.

Then when his friends came over, he'd welcome them with open arms, charm them with jokes, and prop up my mom by showering her with compliments hours after he showered her with bruises. The idea of family felt like a lie, and I never got over it. Every once in a while, I still relapse to my childhood state, cutting myself off from the world, hiding in my room, questioning everything I know about why we're here, taking solace in the fact that one day it all stops.

I hated my dad's friends, a bunch of Chinese dudes with blue blockers, Jheri curls, and finger rings walking around our house eating our shit, picking their teeth, singing American songs in incomprehensible Chingrish. But this hate was misdirected.

I actually like Jheri curls. I accidentally speak Chingrish frequently and I have many finger rings. There's nothing wrong with any of it. It was a false corollary. Until recently—when I was able to separate the root from the evil—I purposely dressed down my apartments, my speech, and my appearance with metaphorical shit that's defiant in its idiosyncrasy, like the collection of OJ T-shirts I wear on dates, because when I was growing up in the Huang house, impressing friends meant your mom got beat.

Connie was as innocent as Jheri curls and finger rings. None of this was her fault, but in legal terms we'd say that you have to accept the victim as you find him. I'm an eggshell plaintiff with a pre-existing aversion to clean homes, ambience, and patriarchy. The ideal Taiwanese housewife was staring me in the face—well, the ideal actually had its ass turned to me with "Rack City" on, but you know what I'm saying. Wifey was in the building, so I left.

I was scheduled to fly to Miami for an event. I had to wake up early in the morning to catch the flight. Connie knew I had an early morning, so she was spending the night at her apartment on the Upper West Side. It was around 11 P.M. and I was getting ready when she texted me.

> I think I have the flu. I'm so sick right now.

> Drink water, get some rest, take Theraflu.

I assumed she'd had the flu before.

> I'm going to the hospital.

> Damn, girl, it's like that?

> I'm puking everywhere. Twice already. It's really bad.

> ECK,* don't hurt nobody with that, lol.

> I'm going to come down to the hospital by you.
> Will you come with me?

> I'm not trying to be insensitive, but there's a hospital on the Upper West Side near you, and you know I gotta catch a flight in the morning.

> Fine.

I went to sleep.

Two hours later, our intercom buzzer goes off. Evan answered it and then walked over to my bed.

"Yo, Connie is here."

"What? Are you serious?"

---

* Pusha T ad-lib.

"Yeah, I just buzzed her in."

"Fuck my life."

I opened the door and there she was, disheveled, her face red, wearing a USC hoodie.

"I just went to the hospital down the street, waited for two hours by myself, and still didn't get seen by a doctor!"

"Yo, why are you here if you didn't see a doctor?"

"Because I'm sick and I don't feel good!"

Evan intervened.

"Connie, sit on the couch, I'll get you some Theraflu."

"Thank you, Evan! Geez, at least someone is a gentleman here."

I was about to kill Evan. Son brought out a Home Depot bucket full of hot water and some sort of Aveeno chicken pox powder situation that has absolutely no effect on the flu. He got her a hot towel for her head and a blanket. The two of them should've opened a bed and breakfast together.

"I puked three times tonight and you never even showed up to the hospital!"

"I don't see you puking now."

"Do you think I'm lying?"

"I just think you're being dramatic. It's the fucking flu. People get the flu, they puke, they shower, they sleep, and they go back to work in three days. Nobody goes to the hospital for the flu."

"You are the worst person ever! I can't believe I'm dating somebody like you."

Once she said that all I could think about was Mya on that Silkk the Shocker track "Somebody Like Me." Where is Mya? I love Mya. No one looked better than Mya wearing that Carolina Blue Jordan jersey dress in *Best of Me*. I need somebody like Mya.

"All right, I'm going back to sleep."

I walked past my wall of sneakers and went to bed, hoping that Mya would slide up in my subconscious that night, but Connie kept blowing up my spot.

"You're making me sleep on the couch?"

"Connie, you want me to show you I care and reassure you that I'll be there for you, but you know what, I just met you! I don't want to lie to you. And I have no idea if I'm going to be there for you the next time you have the flu because I don't think it's that serious."

She started crying, and I ignored her. I never asked for any of this. She wanted a relationship, she decided to move herself in, she made me breakfast I never asked for, all because she wanted someone to go to the hospital with her one day when she really needed it. When you're with someone, you're searching the subtexts, looking into their day-to-day actions, their instincts and facial expressions, trying to decode it all to answer the only question that matters: whether they're gonna hold you down. And in her defense, that's what everyone wants. From Jadakiss to DMX to Pac to 50 Cent to Connie, everyone wants a ride-or-die chick, 541ls size 7 in girls, Bonnie & Clyde, with the flu, in the hospital, asking "21 Questions" type relationship. But a girl you've dated for five weeks creating drama to test a ninja in some zero-gravity flu chamber to determine whether this relationship will make it in space is on another one.

The next morning I woke up at 6 A.M., and she was already gone. All her stuff was out the crib, and she left one pair of shoes that I'd bought for her the weekend before. I had to laugh. The girl did everything with two plates. #Extra

A week later, I came back from Miami and she apologized. I had spent a week wondering just how stank and fermented my soul had become, and then *she* apologized. It threw me for a loop. Some sort of Jedi mind trick, but it worked. Of course, once she retreated a little, I apologized and told her I'd make more of an effort to let her know I cared, but I only cared because I thought Connie was good for me. In the most selfish way, I kept seeing Connie because on paper it made sense.

My brother liked her, my mom would love her, and I should have wanted a compliant, fly Taiwanese-Chinese chick who could cure my bronchitis with a futuristic cousin of ginseng, but my life goal wasn't to live forever with the prettiest handmaiden in the Five Kingdoms.

For weeks, Connie kept bothering me to go to brunch. I hate brunch.

Bags, open-toed sandals, sundresses, strollers, and for what? EGGS! Everybody wants some cot damn EGGS.

But there I was at brunch. Connie sat across from me with these huge obnoxious Armani sunglasses and a *Rhythm Nation*–esque hat. I kept asking myself why she had a South Beach look in North Fort Greene and had no answer. Halfway through these sideways thoughts, she spoke.

"You know, there are no good restaurants in New York."

I was confused.

"What do you mean, there are no good restaurants in New York?"

"There just aren't any good veggie restaurants."

"That's a big statement."

"Well, I don't like any of them."

"There are tons of good restaurants in New York. What is your favorite restaurant in L.A.?"

"I like eating my mom's food."

"Your mom is not a restaurant. Unless your mama's so fat that she's Fat Burger."

"My mom isn't fat, she's a vegetarian, too. You know, you're mean."

"I'm not mean! You make no sense."

"I think I make sense, you're just mean."

My dick was going to kill me, but I had to end it. "Rack City" was a great song, but it was a five-weeks-in-the-club song, and it had been eight weeks already.

"I don't think this is fun anymore."

"I don't think it's fun, either, but I still like you."

"I'm sorry. I'm not trying to be mean, but I just don't think I'm ready for all this."

Neither of us said anything for about ten minutes, and then I asked for the check. There was no sadness in her face; no sign of crying. She was going to be better off without me, and I think she knew it.

For three months, I didn't hear from Connie. I never reached out, and neither did she. One night, I got home from a bar, turned on my computer, and saw an email from her.

I miss u like mad and I hate that I do. I hate that I feel this way and I hate that I feel like I'm the only one that does.

Finally, I realized what was wrong. She liked me and missed me, but there was no logical reason to miss someone who doesn't care about you, and she knew it. She didn't like me or miss me; she just *needed* someone — anyone. I understood it. I was looking for someone, too. It just wasn't Connie.

I wrote her back.

Hey. It's 2:42 A.M. and I think you were just having one of those nights ha ha. I want to be honest and not lead you on or be unfair but I don't feel the same way. You shouldn't miss me because I'm no good for you.

It's my dumb luck that I was disappointed early in life. I never saw my parents kiss until late in high school. They rarely said "I love you," and I'm pretty sure I saw my dad hit my mom before I saw them hug. They had rings, they had kids, they had a clean crib, and they had cars, but they didn't have love. I wasn't goin' out like that. I was determined to know love.

Dena

Three months after I broke up with Connie, I threw a party for my boy Sparkz on the rooftop at the Hotel Williamsburg. Sparkz was moving from New York to Berlin and grew up a Mobb Deep fan, so Prodigy blessed us with a performance on the bar in denim shorts. I fux with P because he believes in spaceships and loves P. F. Chang's, but also stunts on people at Red Lobster by ordering lobster, not eating said lobster, and just dipping cheddar biscuits in the butter because he can. One day, I would like to do all of these things.

Somewhere between "Shook Ones" and "Drop a Gem on 'Em," it started to rain. People started running and screaming like the Feds were coming through, but the panic was entirely created by the prospect of wet streetwear.

"IT'S RAINING AND I'M WEARING VISVIM!!!"

"WHITE SUPREME BOX TEE NIPPLE FAIL!"

"MY OPENING CEREMONY FEEL SOME TYPE OF WAY ABOUT THIS."

"HOOD BY RAIN."

"COMMES DES FUCK DOWN!"

"EVERYBODY GO TO THE TURKEY'S NEST!"

"TURKEY'S NEST!"

"TO THE TURKEY'S NEST!"

"PLEASE EXIT IN AN ORDERLY FASHION, GO TO THE TURKEY'S NEST, AND DON'T STEP ON MY SOUTH BEACH 'BRONS."

"PEOPLE WITH ASICS EXIT LAST, YOUR SHOES ARE WORTHLESS."

After everyone dispersed to the Turkey's Nest, I found Prodigy and his manager, Marvis, downstairs.

"Ayo, E, what kind of spot is this, b?"

"Williamsburg dive bar. I don't come out here much, but this spot is classic: summertime double cup shit."

"Word? It's like that?"

"Yeah, you can play pool, hang out, take drinks to go if you want. It's low-key."

"Daaamn, we 'bout to get it in, then. Son got the oil."*

To the Nest we went.

It was dark, musty, festive, and the bar seemed like a great place for Blake Lively from *The Town* to pitch oxy. I ordered three double rum and Sprites, then blessed 'em with oil. New York was caught up with the art of mixology, but I found my own rapture watching the codeine slink its way through the ice, hit the bottom, come back a wave of dark brownish red, and extend its tentacles through the rest of my rum and Sprite, the whole drink eventually settling into a perfect shade of eggplant.

I saw Evan and my friend Berto standing nearby between two groups of women. To his right were two white women and to the left were three Asians, who at the moment were being entertained by Evan.

"What's poppin', slime?"

"Drop and slide. Evan is doing work with the Cherry Blossoms so I'm trying to see wassup here."

"I like this. Engaged but still tending the crops."

"BRUH, I'm doing this purely for Evan's benefit."

"Aren't we all?"

I'd already met one of the two women standing with Berto, Sissy, but didn't recognize her friend.

"Wassup, Sissy!"

---

* Codeine promethazine—sizzurp.

"Well, hello, Edwyn, how are you this evening?"

Sissy was a tall white girl with Asiatic eyes who liked overly formal salutations. I think it was her game. Some sort of bohemian *Downton Abbey* seduction that really confused me but got a lot of other people open.

"I'm aight. When'd you guys get here?"

"We tried to get into the party, but they wouldn't let me in!"

I turned to Sissy's friend.

"I'm Eddie, by the way."

"Hey! I'm Dena."

We shook hands.

"You guys put *Sissy* on the list, but I don't have an ID that says Sissy."

"Your parents didn't name you Sissy?"

"No, unfortunately they did not."

"What's your government name?"

"Alicia. Alicia Clemens."

"So, you told them your name was Sissy and they didn't let you in?"

"No, they did not, Edwyn, because I don't have an ID with that name."

"My ID doesn't say Eddie, but they let me in."

"Well, Sissy is quite a departure from Alicia."

"But Sissy isn't a name you just randomly make up on the spot and find on the list. That's like rolling up to a club and asking 'Who wants to sex Mutombo?' You don't need ID if your name is Sissy or Dikembe Mutombo."

"I tend to agree, Edwyn, I really do, but we didn't get in, so we've been drinking wine at the Turkey's Nest ever since."

"Who drinks wine at the Turkey's Nest?"

"We do, Edwyn."

That was Dena.

"Call me Eddie. Sissy likes to do the Edwyn thing, but I don't like Edwyn. It's a coolie name."

"WHAT?"

"Coolie name, you know, government name. It's too English. Eddie sounds like something a Chinaman could have made up at Ellis Island on the spot. It's not like Edwyn, which the system uses to identify me."

"Ha ha ha, you are so strange, but I do like this turquoise situation," she said, eyeing my pullover hoodie–swim trunks set.

"Thanks. I fux with beach formal; just 'cause there's mesh netting on your balls doesn't mean you shouldn't be matching."

She laughed. She had a funny laugh. She would drink wine and laugh into her glass then pull it away from her face. She had mic control with a wineglass, which I found graceful and dopey and disarming at the same time. She looked into my glass.

"What are you drinking?"

"Oh, try some, it's good."

"OK."

She took a sip. I really didn't think too much about it, I was just enjoying the rhythm of the conversation and watching the way she laughed. I figured no need to disclose I was drinking sizzurp too early in the conversation. But I had miscalculated.

"OH MY GOD, what is that?"

"It's just purple drink, you don't like it?"

"Yuck, it tastes like medicine."

"Well, it kind of is medicine."

"Did you just drug me?"

"No, technically you drugged yourself, but it's nothing crazy: codeine promethazine."

"That sounds terrible. What is that?"

"It's like drinking Robitussin, you've taken Robitussin, right?"

"Oh yeah, I love robo-tripping."

"Yeah, same thing, you just put it in a Styrofoam cup, more concentrated formula, with even more of the anti-chest congestion benefits of DM."

"OK, but you still drugged me."

"I accept that."

I figured that could have gone a lot worse, so I got away while I was still ahead and walked to the bathroom. With one hand directing my stream and the other holding my phone, I checked my texts.

What's really good my g? We staying here? —Berto

Hey! We're at Le Bain. Are you still coming? —Caitlin

Noodletown? —Steve

What's poppington? —James

Haiiiiii **emoji** —Tashia

Vibes? Vibes? VASSUP? —Emile

The key to being single in New York is recognizing that no one is really inviting you anywhere. No one is that interested in you, they just need a friend right now, and you really shouldn't catch feelings. I went back to see Dena.

And there she was, laughing with a wineglass by her face again.

"Roberto! Alberto!" she said in an Italian accent.

"Yo, chill!" Roberto said sheepishly.

"What's so funny, y'all?"

"Did you know Berto's name is Roberto Alberto Martinez?"

"Motherfucker, your name is Roberto Alberto?"

"YES! My name is Roberto Alberto! What's the big deal?"

"Homie, you're like the dude Montego Montoya from *Princess Diaries*."

Dena bent in half in laughter.

"You mean Inigo Montoya from *Princess Bride*?"

"Yeah! You know what I'm talking about. You the ninja from *Princess Bride*."

"Oh my god, you two are so goofy: Roberto Alberto and Montego Montoya."

I can't remember what she was wearing. At that point, I couldn't really hear what she was saying, I had drunk so much sizzurp. But I remember telling myself: "This is good. This is fun. I like it."*

I also couldn't "figure out" what she looked like. I could obviously see what she looked like, but it was a very particular look that I couldn't figure out because she kept moving. There was this big glass in front of her face, her hair was moving, and she kept laughing. Being the superficial, insecure, thirty-year-old male that I was, all I cared about was whether she was attractive, and I couldn't fucking figure it out.

"You're kinda quiet over there, Montego. What's going on?"

"I dunno. I think it's this drink."

"You should really stop drinking cough syrup. It's a middle school thing."

I couldn't respond. I was just staring at her, squinting and tilting my head, thinking to myself: "What the hell does this girl look like?"

After a few awkward seconds, I thought, Fuck it.

"Yo! What's your number?"

"Ohhh, you want my number?"

"Yeah. You're funny. I want to call you."

"OK. Gimme your phone."

A few hours later, I was in a hospital waiting room eating takeout pancakes from IHOP, waiting for my fifty-year-old homie to get stitched up after he fought the young and reckless DJ at Le Bain, when Sissy texted me.

Do you like Dena?

She's cool.

I think she likes you.

---

* James White is a Chinese Vine star who is on a search for a white wife; he ends many of his Vines with the tag "I like it."

She got good taste.

Are you going to ask her out?

YES SISSY! I am going to call her.

That's great, Edwyn.

I texted her, and we planned to meet five days later for a date. I had never been more lukewarm about a date. I wasn't ready.

For years, my dating technique had degraded. Six years of my adult life were committed to Ning, the months after were spent trying to figure out what happened, then I took my turn in the assembly line pounding chicken thighs for a year before I met Connie. Over a decade of my life, I'd been single for fewer than eighteen months, including the last three. Every time I tried to get free, someone pulled me back in.

I liked being in relationships, but I couldn't figure out what I needed at that point. I'd had a few OKCupid-brokered dates and I'd told myself to stay free, but here I was committing to a meal at a set time before 8 P.M. with an actual person I'd met at a bar the old-fashioned way, not using the hotness filter on the drop-down menu or a computer's compatibility projection. I talked to Evan about it.

"Yo, I should cancel this date."

"What are you talking about?"

"I can't remember what she looks like."

"How do you not remember? She was taller than you, skinny, and had a sharp nose."

"She had a big nose, huh?"

"She had a big nose, but you like that."

"I do like that.* But she's skinny. I don't like that."

---

* I used to jerk off watching *The Nanny* when I was a kid. What up, Fran Drescher? Love you, ma.

"Then don't go on the date! It's just a date. It's not the end of the world."

"She was funny, though. I remember that."

"She was funny. You drugged her and she didn't report you and she liked that Roberto is Roberto Alberto. We've known Berto for eight years, and we had no idea. She's investigative."

"Was she hot?"

"Sure. She was hot. She's definitely hot enough to go on a date with."

"Phil said she was fat."

"Phil is a hater. She's not fat."

"I like fat, though."

"SO WHY ARE YOU ASKING? GO ON THE DATE, NUMB-NUTS."

"Fine. It's a good excuse to wear Visvims."

"Yes, wear those stupid Japanese shaman shoes you spent two hundred and fifty dollars* on."

I have to call myself out. I have spent *decades* of my life sitting around thinking about whether the girl I'm dating is good-looking enough. I've spent equal time thinking about whether I'm good-looking enough as if there's some sort of PER† for humans playing the game. I have no idea if this is normal behavior, but I have to tell you it is an inexcusable waste of time.

I was slightly less late than she was by a few seconds so she crept up behind me, grabbed my dump truck, and made a predator face. I liked it. Right on cue, the hostess led us to our table at this now-shuttered Hawaiian restaurant which, as it turned out, had horrible warm poke and terrible drinks. I asked a friend from Hawaii for the recommendation

---

* Visvim early adopter, pre–Emile Haynie, pre–John Mayer $450 prices.

† This dude John Hollinger has this system that takes into account everything a basketball player does on the court and tries to spit out one single Player Efficiency Rating. The idea that all your contributions on a court (or a planet) can be captured by one number and then contrasted against everyone else's number is interesting, insulting, and humbling—if inaccurate.

because I was on a piña colada kick, but this spot was not an unknow-
ingly shitty Hawaiian restaurant that still thought tiki drinks were pop-
pington, but a serious restaurant seemingly inspired by Cameron Crowe's
Hawaii.

I regretted not going to L&L BBQ, but as soon as Dena sat down
across from me in her tan-crème polka-dot button-down blouse and
black shorts with combat boots, I thought, Interesting, she's going with
the militant covered up look. I have rubbed cocoa butter into stretch
marks thinking they were the female Rosetta stones whispering the history of woman to me like iliotibial band* Braille, but none of those
stretch marks said as much to me as Dena's polka-dot blouse. She looked
smart, alluring, but not here for hook-ups. I liked it, but I wasn't ready.
The ignorant fifteen-year-old in me wanted to throw the fight, spit game
like Cassidy in "Hotel," and tell my boys she was a bitch when I got
home. It can't hurt me if I set it on fire first, I thought.

"Hi!"

She interrupted my spiraling thoughts.

"Hi."

"So we're here. This is exciting, ha ha."

"Ha ha, where'd you come from?"

"East Harlem."

"Word, you on your Immortal Technique. Is that why you wear combat boots and oversized shorts?"

"No. I wear these shorts because THEY FIT ME."

"You live up there?"

"Yeah, I love East Harlem. It's a real neighborhood."

"It's also far enough from Red Rooster."

"What's Red Rooster?"

"It's a terrible restaurant politicians go to so they can say they support
black people, not really engage black culture, say hello to Don Lemon,
and then get back into their town cars without incident because it's on
the Ave."

---

* The IT band is on your thighs, ma.

"Interesting. You really don't like this place, but you know a lot about it."

"Yeah. When I don't like something, I go out of my way to count the ways."

"It's not worth your time. You should just ignore it."

This surprised me. My self-aware Costanza-condition joke usually got a laugh.

"I shouldn't ignore it, though. People should be aware why they go to this shit restaurant, and we shouldn't be down with credit-card liberalism."

"Or you can just let them have that shit restaurant and focus on what you care about. Lead by example." She smiled as she lectured. I liked that.

I changed the subject to something that was more likely to lead to witty banter and, most important, sex.

"Did you have fun at the party last week?"

"Yeah, I enjoyed being drugged." Fuck, this one wasn't going to lead to the honey hole, either.

"I mean, a guy buying you a drink with no expectations is nice. A guy giving you the shirt off his back is better. But a guy who gives you his drink *with* codeine promethazine in it is prescriptive."

No response from her until she changed the subject.

"Where are you from?"

"D.C., Orlando, I did a one-year bid in Pittsburgh, back to Orlando 'cause it was just that fucking awesome, and then eight years in New York now."

"Where does your family live?"

"They're in Orlando."

"Do you have brothers and sisters?"

"Two brothers. One lives with my parents, the other lives with me. Hopefully you will meet him at my apartment later."

"Ohhhhh, I get it. That was supposed to be funny."

"I try."

There was silence as I tried to think about what to say next that could turn us back toward the honey hole, but I had nothing. So I succumbed to logic and asked a question that followed reasonably after hers.

"What about your family?"

"I'm glad you finally asked."

She laughed . . . and I was relieved. Not because she laughed but because she was in control.

"They all live in Scranton. Younger brother, younger sister, I got my grandparents on my dad's side, they're the best."

"You go back a lot?"

"Yeah, every other week."

"WHAT?"

"Yeah, I see them every other week."

"You see your parents every other week?"

"Yeah! Why is that so weird? Don't you talk to your parents?"

"I mean, I try not to, but eventually Evan gives me the phone while I'm on the toilet and I talk to my mom."

"That's terrible."

"No, if you met my mom you would understand. She would run my life from a toilet if she could, and she tries. Once a month. When Evan gives me the phone."

"You should really call your mother more."

Some women are Jedi. Dena was the type that even if she wasn't interested, she'd split the bill, give you advice in passing, smile, wink, and let you charge it to the game. Effortless control is maddeningly attractive.

"So what do you do?"

"I cook food at this restaurant in the East Village."

"What restaurant?"

"It's a small Taiwanese sandwich shop. We make pork buns and stuff."

"What's a pork bun?"

I was so happy that she had no idea. Baohaus was celebrated, my memoir was finished, and in a week I'd be shooting the first episode of my show for Vice. I'd wanted it all, but everything burned brighter in this new terrain. The only skin I'd ever known was peeling. Someone had to know me before it was all gone, before I was all brand new . . .

"It's like a Taiwanese taco or hamburger with pork. It's whatever."

"Do you like it?"

"Yeah, I love cooking. It gets boring making the same dish over and over, but when I figure new things out about it, I really like it."

"What is it you like about cooking, though?"

I used to be quick with this one, but after the last few years, constantly talking about food, it felt mechanical.

Dena was cool, though, and I didn't want to put up another wall. If anyone was going to know *me*, I had to remember how it used to feel. I found my center and let Dena in.

"I'm tired of cooking, but I still love it. When it's done right, cooking is art in the most accessible, immediate, and satisfying way. Anyone can do it, anyone can appreciate it, and it's extremely democratic. It doesn't cost me much in terms of money or time, there doesn't have to be pageantry, but it can give you a lot. I can express anything with food. When it's done really well, it's the perfect manifestation of existence. I mean, what else in the world literally sustains us and represents us all at the same time?"

She stirred her drink, bit the straw, and smiled. I'd revealed too much.

"You're a smart one, aren't you?" she said, sizing me up.

"It's relative. By definition, morons wipe standing up."

"You wipe standing up?"

"I'm by definition a moron."

The date ran seven hours. We ended up on a bench for an hour, watched *Saturday Night Live* for another two hours in the crib, and after the first thirty minutes I never thought about making a move. It was the date I'd always wanted in high school. Back then, I'd talk to girls about family, about the "essence," and how I was gonna flip the script on the world 'cause I bumped my head as a child.* It led to incredible first

* Flipmode is the greatest. Holla at Baby Sham. Holla at Spliff Star. Holla at Rah Digga. Busta you cool.

dates, no hand jobs, and the friend zone. Once I got to know these girls, I didn't want to go hard in the paint, and they thought I wasn't interested. I respected them.

And while I'd spent the last six months making up for it, attacking anything that moves, dunkin' on girls like Darryl Dawkins, it wasn't fulfilling. Why would you want to dominate someone? Why would you want to control someone? Alfred Hitchcock had it wrong. It's not about choppin' these women down in the shower, attacking them with birds, or poking your phallic camera through the rear window. I knew this much.

But I was too scared to go back to the idealistic juvenile who had nothing in his possession but a moral compass and a hard-on. Those days before women were just bodies and condoms were just bags. Like Macbeth contemplating a sea of blood—looking back at a gang of noncompostable latex washed up on the shore—I turned and walked farther into the sea. I tied up my timbs to make sure I didn't slip, pulled out my smif-n-wessun and went in to catch wreck.[*]

The next day, I played everything back in my mind. Usually I'd be basking in the glow of a win, but I discovered there are games in this world that are inexplicably not basketball and take nonlinear forms. I was confused. On her way out she told me that she'd had fun and that she'd call. But she left in record time and didn't even wait for me to close the door behind her. I got Billy Crystal'd.[†] When things went wrong in those days, I blamed Evan.

"Evan . . . I need a door."

"How are we going to put a door in the living room, my g?"

"I dunno, but I think I bugged Dena out by not having a door."

"You didn't bug her out not having a door. You're bugged out because you think it's a big deal that she didn't try to stay over."

---

[*] Smif-n-Wessun, "Timz N Hood Chek."

[†] *When Harry Met Sally.*

"Aren't they supposed to try to stay over?"

"Some stay, some go, what are you gonna do?"

"If they're into it, they all try to hang out for a little. Remember that girl from North Carolina that made me take her back out for a drink in SoHo?"

"She was a tourist! You brought her back at like eleven and she didn't want to go back to her hotel. Plus, when Connie stayed and then left her stuff you got all paranoid."

"Fam, it's definitely some trap house shit that I have a bed in the living room and you walk through my dates."

"I'm not 'walking through your dates.' I'm walking to the kitchen or I'm walking to leave the apartment."

"But you have to walk through my date to do that!"

"Since when are these 'dates'? This shit is less personal than buying falafel at Murray's."

"You don't understand my situation."

"Are you listening to yourself? Your situation is that you don't have a door to your room and I walk by sometimes when people don't have clothes on. Big deal!"

"I hate you."

"Whatever, man, I'll get you curtains to divide your mattress from the rest of the living room."

"Fine."

Evan was in many ways the lord of the apartment. I gave him the bigger room, he made slightly more logical interior choices, and he actually had motor skills. I paid for everything, and he installed it.

"What kind of curtains do you want?"

"Polo." He looked at me like a crazy person, but being the Generation Y-er that he was, he consulted the internet before assuming anything was crazy.

"There are a lot of Polo curtains. What kind do you want?"

"Snow Beach."

"Dick, they don't have Snow Beach. They have gingham, plaid, plain, basic shit."

"Casino."

"Yo, I'm not gonna help you if you keep making ridiculous requests. This isn't a Fabolous video."

"It's not ridiculous. Ralph should make Casino curtains. He's basically just assuming that the people who buy Polo Casino shirts don't have homes they want to match."

"I'm buying you gingham."

As Evan got older, he got sick of my requests, stopped finding them humorous, and wanted to be his own man. What he didn't realize was that no one was stopping him but himself. I had a list of complaints about Evan, and he had a corresponding list with my name on it, but I remembered what Dena said about focusing on what I cared about and started to list all the reasons I loved Evan.

Number one had to be his impersonation of the Vietnamese waiters at Pho Banc and number two was probably the fact that he'd picked up all the slack and taken on every single shitty job I didn't want to do. We had a social contract between us and shared a single vision: representing our family, our culture, and our experience through a restaurant serving four-dollar sandwiches. Once the shop took off, I started telling our story in books, interviews, and shows, while Evan ran the core business. I had complaints about how Evan did his job, but at the end of the day, he did it. And I was taking it for granted.

I had to stop. Not just with Evan, but Dena, too. When I cared about someone, I'd start to pick at all the flaws, highlight potential problems, and assume that everything would inevitably unravel. Deep down I just didn't think I deserved anything nice.

Things were different with sports, though. With sports, I believed.

Even after Redskins or Knicks losses when people would tell me, "It's all over," "We should be Ravens fans," "Fuck the Knicks," I genuinely believed that I could still will the Redskins and Knicks to the championship. In the years they didn't win it all (every year), I just told myself I didn't want it bad enough and came back the next year with my helmet strapped on a notch tighter. But—what the fuck do the Redskins and Knicks mean to me? I put more effort into the Knicks and Redskins than anything else in my life and they were BUMS, sucking all my energy and juju into a vortex. Who was I kidding? The Knicks are NEVER going to win the championship, and nothing good should ever happen to Daniel Snyder.

That day I turned in my player pass, canceled my plans, gave Evan tickets to a Knicks game I was taking another girl to, and made a decision. Take all the energy you invest in negative things like Daniel Snyder, James Dolan, and Marcus Samuelsson, and put it back into something worthwhile. I picked Dena.

China

gotta level with you for a second. I wasn't sure why I was going to China. It all started at the press lunch for my first book, when this old head asked me: "*Fresh Off the Boat* is a coming-of-age memoir, a foregone conclusion. What I want to know is what's next?"

This was a common question back then—people want to be on that next shit before they can even shake the sand out their crotch from the first wave. But I scrambled for an answer.

"Well, I think the logical bookend would be to flip it upside down, reverse the family's migration back to China and ask the same questions."

"And what are those questions?"

"I mean . . . it's like the Marvel Comics 'What if?' joints. What if I was born in China? Could I have created my own place in China like I did in America? Can I ever be Chinese again? Are kids like cognac blunt wraps? Could I just honey-dip them in the Chinese wilderness and make us X.O. again?"

"Ha ha, I never thought I'd hear about reverse migration and cognac blunt wraps in the same sentence. Well, good luck."

I made a note to myself, went home that night, and a week later emailed the idea to my editor and Obi-Wan Kenobi, Chris Jackson:

Undercover Brothers (lol, prob not the title, but funny)

I want to go undercover as a bao vendor with my brothers in China. We will go back, make baos, sell them on the street, live with locals, and report. There are multiple layers but I feel like my personal quest is to see how my food and I will be received in China as an American-born Chinese-Taiwanese. There will be struggles to get the business started, learn how to finesse the system. Are there commercial kitchen laws? What are the food and business standards in China and how do they compare to the U.S.? Not on a global Target Beijing to Target Atlantic Ave scale but on a Baohaus to Beijing food cart vendor level. I want people to know what the day-to-day life of a Chinese street cart vendor is. There are all these chefs talking about backpacking in countries, coming back with recipes, then trying to re-create some trattoria or izakaya they found abroad. I'm doing the reverse. I'm not trying to feed White Brooklyn. I'm trying to feed brownish–yellowish–chronic bronchitis Beijing and other cities like it. Classic Eddie Downward Assimilation story.

My dad always said, "When China blows the whistle, its children will come home." I want to know if that's true. Can I claim China? Am I a poser? Can I actually come home and *be* Chinese? What does that even mean?

It sounded good on paper. The book was sold to the publisher in early January 2013, and my tickets were booked for July. But for months, I ignored the business and ignored my plans for China. All the space was filled by Dena.

It was her.

I just couldn't believe it.

Everyone's told you how it's going to happen. At first sight, at third sight, at last sight, out of sight . . . but when it's real, it's got nothin' to do with sight. It's out of body and you just ride it. That's what I was feeling thirty thousand feet in the sky, flying over the Mongolian steppe, eating a bag of cocktail peanuts, watching *Crazy, Stupid, Love*. She wasn't even with me, but I knew. I couldn't wait to tell her.

As a man that usually went Ric Flair, in this case I went Rick Ross. #TearsOfJoy running down my face listening to Gosling tell Emma

Stone how he always wanted a friend. Someone he didn't have to seduce and smash and then passive-aggressively ask to leave. Someone to share fluids with, then eat dried plums from Ten Ren Tea while watching *Knicks in 60* because the only way to enjoy the Knicks is with wifey, sipping from a plastic mug full of high mountain oolong tea, exchanging sweet nothings as J. R. Smith goes 0 for 19 on the way to another epic night at Greenhouse.*

Dena was from Scranton, a.k.a. Dunder Mifflin headquarters, and her Scranton-ness connected us. People from Scranton are similar to Chinese Americans in this way: They don't expect anything good to happen to them. They believe in hard work, but not because they expect any tangible positive results. They suspect that their hard work and sacrifice will most likely disappear into the ether somewhere between Pittsburgh and Philadelphia, but that's no excuse to stop trying. Just because you're neither Pittsburgh nor Philadelphia doesn't mean Billy Joel isn't going to write a song about you one day, and you should always be ready for it. They take pride in their food (Exhibit A: Old Forge Pizza), family, and tradition but are pretty sure that nothing is going to make it better than it was before when it was the Electric City or Middle Kingdom. They had coal, we had opium, and Derek Zoolander tells me they both cause black lung. I was willing to risk it.

Dena had me sprung like *Mystic Pizza* Julia Roberts—her sharp features, flashing smile, and townie vibes got my dick so motherfucking hard. Even after all my years shunning everything suburban and Americana, I couldn't turn my back on a 1980s pizza pie romance because let's face it, there is nothing more romantically exotic to a Chinaman than Julia Roberts, the hooker boots from *Pretty Woman*, and motherfucking pizza. I couldn't deny that this specific slice of Americana was something I wanted to eat the rest of my life.

Wait. *Why do I always do that?* Why did I always reduce attraction to the physical and racial? I had a gift for turning everything in my life into jokes about bodies and bodily functions and race without any conscious

---

* Downtown NY club.

effort or deliberation. It was partly because bodies and bodily functions and racism are real and I never wanted to look away. But part of it was my own fear. The Tao of my life was self-deprecation, but Dena was the first girl I tried not to project my insecurities onto. She never made me feel insufficient or different.

(But when I talk quietly with my homies I still tell those pink nipple jokes. It's a disease. Like eating gummy bears when everyone is asleep and then asking why I have tits in the morning.)

I wondered what Dena was doing at that moment. Knowing her, she was probably flipping through Pinterest,* listening to Nancy Wilson, or eating tacos from a truck in Spanish Harlem, but I hoped she was taking a shit. I genuinely hope she ate a taco and took a shit while her mans was thousands of miles away in a plane crying, eating peanuts, watching Gosling do his thing, telling himself he'd found the one, because for Dena and me, it started with a hurricane and a poop.

After the first few months we were together, I'd try to *accidentally* walk into the bathroom in the morning while she was losing weight. Hurricane Sandy gave us our moment. We'd been dating a solid three months when the hurricane appeared on the horizon. I lured her to the apartment in Stuy Town with visions of Korean hot pot, *Game of Thrones*, and a Swedish foam mattress. For months, we'd hung out a couple times a week, never back-to-back days, nothing official, but I knew. She was playing it very defensively, assuming the worst and never even hinting long-term. But Hurricane Sandy had us locked down. Back-to-back days were inevitable. For days, we couldn't go outside because lower Manhattan was flooded and powerless. After holding it in for a good seventy-two hours, she had to go.

I knew it was going down. How could it not? We ate Korean hot pot over a butane burner three times a day. There was no way she could pretend like she didn't poop! So while she did her work, I knocked on the door.

"I'm in here!"

---

* She loved looking at interiors on Pinterest.

"I gotta shave! Lemme in, Dena."

"I'm busy! Stop it!"

"What are you doing in there? Why can't I just get my razor?"

"Eddie, you never shave. Why do you need to shave right now? You don't even have facial hair."

"I don't have facial hair because I shave it. Lemme in!"

"No!"

"Why?"

"Because I'm busy!"

"Are you pooping?"

"No! I'm straightening my hair."

"Why does your hair smell like poop when it's straight?"

"YES! OK! I'M POOPING, YOU CRAZY. Leave me alone!"

"I want to see."

"You are so WEIRD! What is wrong with you? Just let me poop, boo."

"Why are you so weird about pooping? I poop twice a day, and it's great. It's the only time I can talk to my mom."

"That's true, you do talk to your mom in the bathroom. . . . Why?"

"Because the feeling of wasted time is relative to the other things you could be doing at that moment. If I'm on the toilet, I don't feel like I'm wasting time when she asks me the same useless questions every day, but if I was in a cab where I could watch Sandy Kenyon review movies instead of talking to her, I feel like life is passing me by on the phone. . . . Lemme in!"

"You are so annoying, stop it! I don't want you in here!"

I opened the door and there she was, sitting on the toilet, booty spreading off the sides, hair back, face in hands, feet did,* in all her glory.

"Hey, ma, you look great pooping."

"Go awaaay . . ."

"Stop it! This is great. We share everything now."

"What are you talking about? Get out!"

It really wasn't as endearing to Dena as it was to me.

----

* Pedicure.

"OK, OK, I'll go outside. Don't be so hard on yourself. I think it's cool that we can acknowledge you poop."

"GET OUT!"

I left. It was clearly an egregious intrusion of private and psychological space, but I felt like it was necessary. I needed to know I wasn't in love with the mirage, and I needed her to know she could let go of her masks with me. That I wasn't superficial and caught up in her projection of self, but the actual vulnerable, unedited self. We'd been holding back, but we both knew what we were feeling. That day, in the middle of Hurricane Sandy, our feet on the cold tile of my bathroom, it broke open. I was in love.

I know this seems slightly psychotic. It was. I had no idea what unconditional love looked like, so I looked for it in the bathroom. I've heard men and women wax rhetorical: "Will you still love me tomorrow?" "next week?" "next year?" "after I have kids?" Connie had the flu test, but I had the poop test. I thought at the time the poop test was: Could I show her that I love her even with her pants down, at her most vulnerable? Could I show myself? Now I realize the poop test's addendum: would she still love me when I got too close, when I forced vulnerability on her that she wasn't ready for or ever obliged to provide?

That was the beginning. Things went like they do in any other relation-ship on the fast track, and nine months later on that plane to Mongolia, Gosling spoke to me. I imagined hanging out with Dena for the rest of my life, rolling around in aprons with marinara stains, ripping my Polo bedding, feeding each other capicola. And that's when my neurosis kicked in. Yes, I was going to propose. Yes, we would be together forever. Yes, my future wife was from Scranton, but she'd never be Chinese.

I wanted my kids to enjoy capicola too, but what if they turned out like those people at dim sum who only ate shrimp dumplings and crab claws? What if they didn't speak Chinese? What if they put me in a re-tirement home? What if she woke up and decided she didn't like Chinese people one day? What would my mom think? As close as we were, would there always be that distance?

Through the stress and strain, Killa Cam came through and spoke to me as he always does, "What means the world to you?"

And finally, I knew why I was going to China.

Evan

People love Evan. No, wait. People *like* Evan. In fact, everybody likes Evan. They like him because they know him just enough to like him and you start to wonder if that's how he likes it.

Fifteen months after the Connie experiment and a year after meeting Dena,* I arrived in Chengdu Airport after a week of following goats and camels around the Gobi Desert taping a show for Vice. I chose Mongolia for the show because it's the least densely populated country in the world. Considering I'd spent the last eight years chasing cabs and anything in leggings, it was nice to be with goats. You know what you're getting with them: poop and cashmere. I didn't have to chase goats like I chased money and apple bums. With goats, you just gotta be around. Eventually, if they stop to eat enough grass, you can walk among them. That's the best way to get to know something. I tell the kids at Baohaus, if you wanna learn something, walk with me. Walk with me to the train; walk with me to the storage unit; walk with me to the first day of class. Walk with a motherfucker so someone can walk with you.

I loved the city when I was walking, but then you see people running

---

* In the twelve months I knew Dena, I tried shit I'd never done before, like surfing, visiting Scranton, giving white people a chance, and not watching the Knicks. I watched fewer Knicks games than I ever had in my life, but then got sucked in again when it looked like Melo was going to carry us past the Pacers or like Chris Copeland was going to be the second coming of Sam Perkins or like Raymond Felton was actually a decent human being. None of these things were true. Raymond Felton is actually a *terrible* human being, Chris Copeland is a bum, and Melo carried us about as far as I got surfing.

and you put your Air Maxes on, too. You start running, you get thirsty, and then you start chasing. You might get what you want, but it's a blur, because you can't stop running. You forget what you were chasing in the first place and then you die. You can't win; the idea of winning is faker than white meat at KFC. But how am I gonna survive if I'm not 1st in line on 1st Ave. at the 1st National Bank so I can fly 1st class?*

Evan pulled up in a green cab with yellow racing stripes. Luxurious. "Yo, Ed!"

Still smiling. Son could be an hour late and he'd stay cheesin'. It made me smile, too, but I kept it to myself. Evan had mastered walking with people. He liked being on the flank, he never chased, he never ran, and he never really worried. He was happy to be second or third into the fray and pick off what you'd left behind.

"Why you always late, man?"

"I was watching the flight and then there wasn't an update so I just waited for you to call me before I left. Then googin-face† over here got lost."

"How does a cab driver get lost going to the airport?"

"Dude! You're in China, relax."

That was his safe word when I went Dad: relax.

I worried about Evan because he never chased anything. I know that seems like a contradiction, but peep game. People are naturally thirsty. We get hungry, we get horny, we need things. So of course, you tell people slow down, walk with me, nah nah chill. You tell Kobe to pass the rock 'cause son was born thirsty, but LeBron is a god that has to be told Delonte West is a mortal who under no circumstances should be given the ball or introduced to your moms.‡ I'd drop maxims on Evan like "There's no free lunch," "Things aren't just gonna fall in your lap," "The only way is hard work," but I knew I was wrong. Not because I didn't

---

*   Starang.

†   Mouth breather.

‡   People allege that Delonte West slept with LeBron's mom, but in fact HE DID NOT. Poor Delonte, please bring him back to the NBA.

work hard but because Chris Bosh walks among us. Evan knew I was wrong, too.

"How's it been?"

"I've been eating at KFC for three days. Everything else makes me sick. I found a Din Tai Fung today in the mall, though, so I ate there twice."

"I drank fermented horse's milk in the Gobi Desert and then wiped my ass with socks in Ulan Bator."*

"Ugh . . . it's not that bad here. But I saw people pulling up to street stands with a side of pork on the back of a moped, so I stay at the KFC."

We loaded everything into the cab: eighteen pairs of shoes, thirty-two outfits, Dri Fit boxer briefs for weeks. I made small talk with Evan for a good six minutes. Mouth moving, head nodding, but my consciousness out to lunch. Over the last four years, that's what started to happen. Neither of us made sense to the other, neither of us wanted to be around the other, and we did this boss-employee, big brother–younger brother small talk dance.

"How's OKCupid treating you?"

"Great."

"Good."

"Mom wants you to call."

"Awesome, thanks, man."

"Cool, thanks, man."

"No problem, man."

We sounded like bros rather than brothers when we fell into passive aggression, "fantastics" and "greats" dropped in between the "hey, mans."

---

* Fermented mare's milk is known to flush the system, but it was not known to me at the time. I drove from the desert, boarded my flight to Ulan Bator, and upon arrival my water broke. I ran around the airport like a goat with its head cut off, looking for anything to take a shit in. Luckily, I found a men's bathroom. *Unluckily,* this bathroom was in the Ulan Bator airport, had no doors on any stalls, nor did it have toilet paper or toilet seats for human sitting. Every seat had Jackson Pollocks on it, so I had to pop a squat *over* the toilet, made a mudslide, then wiped my ass with my socks. Luckily . . . there was soap.

Something about two passive aggressive Asian Americans in Chengdu echoed post-collegiate whiteness in Murray Hill. I didn't like it.

My mom used to tell us:

"One chopstick: I break you.

"Two chopsticks: tougher, but eventually, I break you.

"Three chopsticks: if you stick together, unbreakable."

That's why our parents had three kids; it's also why I just picked up three chopsticks and broke the shits. Because the things that sound good and help you sleep at night aren't fucking true. They sound good precisely because they aren't true.

"Love conquers all."

Sounds great. Not true.

"HPV is so common that nearly all sexually active men and women will get at least one type of HPV at some point in their lives."*

Sounds horrible, but true.

"Your family will always be there for you."

I wonder. Evan came up to New York from Orlando to help me open Baohaus. He's always been there for me. I had an idea, and he believed in it. When he first offered to join me, back when the idea was still just an idea, it didn't entirely make sense to me.

"I'll help you."

"I'll give you fifty percent of the business!" I countered.

"It's not about the money. I just want to help you."

"But I don't want the help for free."

"But I don't want to be paid."

"You have to be paid. If you work, you should be paid, and if I don't pay, I'm not going to get what I need."

"Dude, I just want to help. You're my brother."

"Fine, but at work we aren't brothers. We're partners."

---

* cdc.gov/std/hpv/stdfact-hpv.htm.

"We're always going to be brothers."

"No, I know, but trust me. At work, we're partners."

Before long our ideas started to diverge. Someone was offering us money for the store and the brand.

"We should sell Baohaus to the group."

"Fuck that. They're offering us half of what we make in a year for twenty-five percent of the company FOREVER."

"I'm tired, man."

"You're twenty-four, you're not supposed to be tired. I'm thirty, let's go!"

"Yo, I'm the one opening and closing the shop, I'm the one working the register. I'm tired."

"I came up with the idea, I put up the money, I do all the recipes, I control the food, I do the press, I manage the business. Someone has to work the day-to-day. You get half!"

"I don't want half! I don't want to open another restaurant. I don't want to do this shit the rest of my life."

"You aren't going to do it the rest of your life if we open another one, make more money, and hire middle management. Then you'll be doing what I'm doing, and we all move up."

"Yeah, but then we'd have to *open another restaurant*! And you're writing the book, doing the show, I'm gonna end up doing everything but the cooking myself. I can't look at another petty cash record or bank statement. I'm twenty-four, I should be exploring the city and doing really reckless irresponsible shit!"

"So you want us to sell Baohaus to these internet cornballs because you want to go do reckless irresponsible shit?"

"No, dickhead, you know I'm not going to go apeshit crazy. I'm just saying, this is my time to be a kid, and I'm sitting here looking at your fucking bank statements all day."

"Fine, Evan, I'll do the bank statements."

"You can't do the bank statements, 'cause you have to finish the fucking *epic* story of your life and our family. So I do the bank statements and everyone is happy, but this is it. I'm not opening another restaurant."

You're probably wondering why we didn't just hire someone. Well, that was the plan I discussed with my mom. I was probably on the toilet at the time.

"Mom, I gotta hire a manager."

"You idiots running a sandwich shop need MANAGER? Give me a break, kidding yourself! You sell three sandwich, have four hundred fifty square feet, MANAGER? Where you put manager? You can't fit other person behind the counter!"

"Yo, we sell eight hundred of those fucking sandwiches every Friday and Saturday, it's not like we run a bodega with cats on the counter."

"What you talk bodega? Why you talk about Spanish food or cat? I don't say Spanish, I say you sell three sandwich and your stupid ass need manager."

"Mom, Evan doesn't want to do this shit anymore. He's burned out. He wants to quit, and I don't blame him. We need a manager."

"Fine, you go hire manager, what have to do with me, but you ask me, I tell you: stupid ass. Two of you should have no problem run this store. And don't you ever trust anyone look at money besides Evan. Even manager, Evan still watch the money."

I used to look at Chinese restaurants and think, Why does every family have to own one? You walk down a block in Chinatown and there are five restaurants on every block serving the same Cantonese food with the same price, quality, and indistinguishable atmosphere. They pay similar rents, buy from the same purveyors, and fight for the same customer. It's bad business for everybody. They should consolidate, diversify offerings, and maximize real estate instead of cutting each other off at the knees with a price war.

The problem with Chinese restaurants is that the employees are family. The lady at the register isn't just a lady at the register, it's your aunt. The server isn't just a server, it's your cousin. The bookkeeper isn't just a bookkeeper, the bookkeeper is your mom. No one gets fired, but everybody fights because you eat, sleep, and shit family. You can't scale up and grow because you can't hire management from the outside. You are stuck with your cousin as the head server even if he's a thirty-five-year-old

virgin who still greets a table with "Haro, prease." Your family is the government, the economy, and the workforce. Come to think of it, the family is communist. And I don't mean that in a negative way. I just mean
there are a lot of slanted-eyed Chris Boshes on the payroll.

Finally, our Chengdu cab driver spoke to us, in Mandarin, of course.

"You Chinese?"

"Yeah, Chinese."

"But you speak English."

"We were born in America."

"Ahhh, I knew it. I can't speak English, but I know good English
when I hear it. You got that smooth English. English is some good shit."

Did he say "good shit"? Nah, but the way he said what he said could
only be translated as an emphatic "good shit." These are the calculations
I make when traveling in China. I register the literal definition of the
word, listen to the emotional cues, and then find its equivalent in the
Taiwanese-Chinese-American culture I live. And they would reciprocate
when translating my third-grade Taiwanese-Chinese-American attempts
at Mandarin.

"Ha ha, it's all right, I guess."

"Lemme ask you. . . . Does America respect China now? Like, really
respect us . . . as a country and people."

"Growing up, no, they laugh at us. They still laugh at us. But because
of the economy, they fear the future."

"Ahhh, I understand. But fear is not the same as respect."

"Absolutely not. It's not even close."

"One day they'll respect us, I know it."

We traded off like Jadakiss and Styles P as Chengdu breezed past my
window, but I watched the driver's eyes through the rearview mirror.

"Do you like America, though?" I asked.

"No, I don't like Americans or Japanese. But then I think . . . people
all the same! Go out of town, first thing you learn is to curse at people.

FACK U! Argentina, Dubai, India, I've been to them all. Everywhere, FACK U! . . . Oh, but I have another question."

"Yeah, go ahead."

"Airport. How do I say airport in English?"

"Airport."

"Ahhh, air pert."

"No, airport."

"Air put."

"No, air port."

"Air poot."

"Yeah, air poot. You got it, homie."

"Ahhh, good, now I don't have to flap my wings when I try to say air poot."

"Are Americans rude to you when you can't communicate?"

"Nah, they get it. You know, today, America still big brother. Right? I welcome them."

The arm-flapping cab driver pulled up to the Soho Building at 60 Kehua Bei Lu right next to ATV Karaoke and across from a giant hot pot restaurant the size of Macy's. I got out of the cab with my big blue hippo suitcase, a lopsided old Victorinox* box on wheels, and a Bart Simpson drawstring backpack. Within seconds, I was bumrushed.

"*Da gu! Da gu!*" (big brother, big brother)

"*Xiong di! Xiong di!*" (my brother, my brother)

"*Shwai gu! Shwai gu!*" (suave brother, suave brother)

"*Lai ba, lai ba!*" (come on, come on)

The three peons came dressed in belly-out tank tops, jeans embroidered with metaphysical animals (e.g., dragons & phoenixes), black cowboy shirts with rhinestones, and the requisite knock-off straight leg Lees. They swarmed from all sides, forcing escort trading cards into our hands, faces, pockets, and luggage. Designed in the exquisite style of early '00s online pornography pop-ups, the cards had naked photos of bright-

---

* Ferris Bueller, what's really good?

skinned Chinese women on one side, stats and phone numbers on the other. It was like arriving as a scout on the banks of Hooker Normandy Beach.

This was the entrance to our "hotel." Three months ago, we had booked rooms online at a place called Hakka Homes, run by someone named Hakka Heather, but upon arrival I remembered that everything you see on the internet is not in fact true.

"Evan, what happened to Hakka Homes?"

"This is Hakka Homes."

"This is Tower A of the Super 8."

"You'll see."

Evan already had my keys, so we bypassed the lobby full of chain smokers and sleeping desk jockeys. It was a common scene in China: the business siesta. No matter where we went, the airport, the hotel, restaurants, people were always sleeping on the job. Morning, afternoon, or late at night, people slept on the spot. Some sitting, head back, mouth wide open, cigarette hangin', others with their hands on the desk, the creative ones creating cots out of cardboard boxes full of quart containers in the prep areas of restaurants. I started taking photos for a coffee table book: *Crouching Tiger, Sleeping Chinaman.*

As I walked through the lobby, I peeped a sign against the wall advertising rooms by the hour. The elevator door opened and the floor was carpeted with sex-worker trading cards and another barker was standing in the corner of the elevator waiting for Johns. Your mans had carpenter shants on and was hotboxing the elevator with Honghe cigarettes, screaming through a gap grill* about his heauxs.

"*Da gu! Da gu! Lai ba!*"

"My g, are we really staying at a Times Square by-the-hour hooker hotel?"

"Yup. We're here."

We walked into a hallway lined with doors, each one fronted by a plastic takeout bag filled with garbage and chopsticks sticking out.

---

* Son had no bottom teeth.

"They pick up garbage every morning if you leave it outside your door."

"There are other people staying here overnight?"

"Yeah, tons of white dudes come in and out for the hookers, but some locals stay here 'cause they work in the area and they're new to town, so they rent from Hakka Homes."

"So what the fuck is Hakka Homes? This is a Super 8!"

"Hakka Heather owns Hakka Homes. She has a deal where she pays Super 8, then 'culturally engineers' the rooms, redecorates them, and rents them to people by the month for more money."

"We're staying at a Chinese hooker Ace Hotel."

"Exactly."

I walked through the hallway and saw a sliding glass door to the balcony with wet laundry hanging. Fifty feet to the right, I reached my room.

I dropped my bags and walked around the room. I was pretty impressed by Hakka Heather's cultural engineering. I was sick of overly curated N.Y., and this badly appropriated motel room was just right. It didn't overtake the culture of by-the-hour hotels and hawker stalls downstairs but lived alongside it wide-eyed and aware of what lay above and below, accepting and confident in its habitat and in its aspirations. Hakka Homes was the rose that grew from a hooker hotel, the answer to the gentrification riddle.

There was a faux Philippe Starck table for two elevated on a stucco platform, which was a little much, but everything else made sense. There was a window overlooking the hood for when you wanted to gaze out at the scooters and hawkers. Refrigerator with freezer, just big enough for dolo living and parties of five. A railroad layout from front door to kitchen to alternate patio door, leading to washing machine and lines for drying clothes. The living room to the left of the railroad structure had cold tile floors that were the perfect complement to the Chengdu blacktop we'd walk every day. I could already imagine my stank-ass feet in Dri Fit socks screamin' for that cold-ass tile on the regular, but the couch had to go. It had been through wars, lumped up, guts falling out, cake-batter-lookin' like Seaman's Furniture. I thought about throwing Saran Wrap on the couch but left it alone.

Out of the corner of my eye, I saw a Doraemon soap dispenser in the bathroom that reminded me of my mom. She loved cartoons. As a kid, I'd be embarrassed that all our household artifacts doubled as animated characters. Soap dispensers, cups, pens, chopsticks, and Kleenex holders in the crib were all green frogs and pink pigs. One of her favorite photos of me was a 1984 joint where I was hanging with a baker's dozen of stuffed animals, hugging Snoopy, lounging on a big red lobster. It was a strange comfort to stand there, a grown-ass man in a Chengdu hooker hotel, half a world away from home, staring at a Doraemon soap dispenser next to a green bottle of Chinese Pert Plus.

I pulled myself out of the moment as Evan and I settled into the room. Something was hanging in the air between us. Evan could tell.

"So what do you want to talk about?" he asked.

"We need to get on the same page."

"I have everything planned. I'm going to get the equipment with Hakka Heather tomorrow. I spoke to her, and she wants to show you options for kitchens, and she is ready for you to cook Friday."

"Yo, that's all good, but I got an email from Dad."

"Yeah, I know."

A month before we came to China, I had sent my dad an email criticizing Evan. For some nonsensical reason, my dad forwarded Evan my email, thinking it'd motivate him or get a conversation started, but it was a miscalculation. The only thing holding Evan and me together was this idea our mother planted in us that family was always enough. If we broke up, it wasn't just the end of our business relationship, but in a lot of ways the end of an ideal. We'd still be brothers, we'd still see each other, but our belief that family always stuck together would die. My parents spoke with Evan; Emery, our other brother, spoke with Evan; everyone felt like it was time for him to leave Baohaus. Except Mom.

My mom had a dream. Ever since she had the three of us, she imagined us working together in the family business. That's how she came up. Whether it was the family mantou, textile, or furniture business, they did it together. The philosophy wasn't unique to my mom's family or Chinese people, but was the universal code of immigrants in general. *All you have is family.* Does being family automatically make you compatible? No. It never did.

The partnership between Evan and me was doomed practically from the beginning, but this ideal of family kept us together for four years. Like alcoholics stumbling through the day on whiskey and trail mix, we were assed out. We had squeezed the family for everything it had, but my mom couldn't let it go because her family had failed, too. She was trying to fix something that broke a long time ago. She saw the mistakes her own family made that shattered their business, and she left Maryland for Orlando when things fell apart. But she studied her family's mistakes, trained us to work together, taught us everything she could in the hopes that we could do it right. That one day her family would stick together.

My pops was ready to let it go. He was the one we called to put Humpty and Dumpty back together every time we broke apart. He ran a restaurant. He knew what the two of us were responsible for, and he knew where the fracture was.

By now I was thirty-one. I wasn't just one of the kids anymore, I had to be a mentor to Baohaus staff. Some of these kids had teen pregnancy scares, others left home, a few dropped out of school, and we had a few guys miss shifts because they got locked up on the weekend. I knew this was normal because I grew up around it. These are the things you sign up for working in a restaurant, but I wanted more for myself, the kids, and of course, Evan.

There was always a division between the college kids working at Baohaus and the career line/prep cooks. You love the college kids because they sell the product well, have email, and they fill out the paperwork. Their phones don't get turned off, their baby mamas don't come to the shop, and their cousins don't try to rob you, but they never last more than a couple semesters, they have wandering eyes, and a lot of times they'll sell your ideas and processes to their next employer. They're carpetbaggers.

On the other side, we had my people from Lefrak City: Rah and Big Chris. They were content with their jobs and genuinely wanted to be friends. There was never any angling to move up or break out. They'd been with us more than three years and even after we let Big Chris go for being late, he kept coming to hang at the shop on the weekends because we were family. We burned Ls and listened to the new Wayne album, never letting business get in the way of what we were. Eventually, Big Chris came back, and he's there today. I actually tell Rah and Big Chris all the time that they gotta take on more responsibility, try to become managers, want more for themselves, but they don't take me seriously. All you need is one person to believe in you, but sometimes it's just too late.

I realized I was in a unique position as a veteran with feet on both sides of the track. I remember being a knucklehead doing ecstasy when I worked at Boston Market and putting my hands in the sweet potato casserole. I was that dude. But I also went to college, went to law school, and built the spaceship. I had a responsibility to these kids, especially Evan.

That was my son. I really felt that way. We lived together and paid our bills together. I woke him up on days he slept in, I had him send me daily recaps of his day, I checked his work, I was way up the motherfucker's ass, and for good reason he got sick of it. But it was all I knew. My father hit Emery and me harder than he ever hit Evan and we were different for it. My personality was a product of an adversarial relationship with my pops—and as in our adversarial judicial system, my truths were many times forged in physical, mental, and social abuse. I learned to take it, I learned to hate it, and I learned to fight back.

On the other hand, Evan was happy. Part of me was relieved that Evan had a chance to see life through clear eyes, but I worried, too. My father was the thug motivation for Emery and me; Evan had to be his own.

"I'm just tired, Evan. I'm really tired."

"I'm tired, too. Dad and Emery both think that we're a bad fit, but Mom is right. We made it this far, we're successful, and we gotta stick together."

Against all logic, I agreed for the simple reason that it sounded good. Leaving home, breaking up, giving up on family, those things sound fucking terrible. I wanted to believe in family; I wanted to believe in love; I wanted to believe in us.

"I agree."

"All right, well, you sleep in. The jet lag is gonna kill you. I'll get up early and meet Hakka Heather for equipment."

"Word. Peace, Ev."

"Later, Ed."

That's how we always left it. A quote for the gods, a pound good night, and a pipe dream that sleep would give us a clean slate the next day.

The empire, long divided, must unite; long united, must divide. Thus it has ever been. *

---

* *Romance of the Three Kingdoms* . . . the book, not the PlayStation game.

Hakka Heather

decided to tell Evan my plan to propose.

"Ev. I need to tell you something."

"What's up?"

"It's important. Sit down."

"Bruh, why so emotional?"

"This is a big deal, man. Extreme life moment."

"Oh. How extreme?"

"Pretty extreme. Defcon One extreme."

"What, are you proposing to Dena?"

I was pissed. How did this fool know?

"WHAT'D YOU SAY?"

"I said, 'ARE YOU PROPOSING TO DENA?'"

"How did you know that?"

"It's so obvious, man. You love that girl."

"What are you talking about? I'm not like crazy in love with her!" I said defensively.

"Uh, genius face, you're proposing to her, how are you not crazy in love with her?"

"Who said I was proposing?"

"OK, so you're not proposing. What am I sitting down for that's extreme Defcon One?"

"Fine, I'm proposing. You're supposed to be surprised, fool!"

"Dude, I live with you. I work with you. I see everything. When you walk sideways and pull the front of your pants, it means you didn't wipe well enough because your dumb ass wipes standing up. Nothing is a surprise anymore."

"I hate you."

"No, you don't hate me, you just mad that I know everything. Especially the fact that you're an idiot that wipes standing up."

"All right. Well, don't tell Mom. I gotta call her."

"That's gonna be fun."

I got nervous.

"Why? What do you think she's going to say?"

"It's Mom. You never know what she's going to say, but it's probably going to be crazy, and she probably wants us all to be single forever even though she tells us to find smart women from wealthy families who are obedient to have children with, she really just wants us to have kids with them and take their money but never actually be happy with anyone but her."

"Damn. You really do know everything. This whole time I thought you were the dumb one."

"Whatever, asshole, my genius constantly goes unnoticed in this family."

I bugged out. I'd been dreading the call because deep down I knew Moms didn't approve of Dena—maybe because she wasn't Taiwanese-Chinese, but primarily because she thought Dena didn't know what she was doing with her life. Dena didn't deny it, and I didn't make a big deal about it. What actual authority did I have to speak on the matter when I was selling weed in a park three years ago? But I knew that wasn't the most promising line of reasoning with my mother.

No, today would not be the day. Mom would have to wait.

Instead Evan and I met Hakka Heather, the owner of Hakka Homes.

Our rally point was downstairs from the Super 8 in front of the store Ha Face. If you forced me to describe it, I'd have to say it was cute. It was fucking cute! What do you want me to say? There were cute women running the store swaddled in versatile fabrics, waving and throwing FOB fingers at everyone who walked by. Their entire collection made no sense, and I loved it. There were elaborate thirty-dollar dresses straight out of a British tea ceremony, others from a rave, and some that were probably intended for the next heaux trading card photo shoot. I couldn't see myself in their psychedelic rompers, but I thought that if I did wear rompers, this is the vision of twenty-one I'd want to be forever. There was so much range and randomness. If there was a proverbial "box" of conventional thinking, they put their kitty kat heels in it and beat it like a Xerox machine from *Office Space*.

Hakka Heather arrived and from one look it was clear she didn't shop at Ha Face. Her brand was her ethnicity: Hakka. Hakka or "guest" people are an ethnic minority that some historians consider to be the "O.C."—Original Chinese—but that's not definitive. Hakka speak Hokkien, make good fish balls, get athlete's foot, and remind me of the Native Tongues posse if the Jungle Brothers had been born in the Chinese Central Plains. They have a different culture than the dominant Han population. You go to a mountain, Hakka people serve their food wearing traditional garments, braid your hair, sell tchotchkes, and act like mystical Chinese unicorn people with healing powers. They send upwardly mobile Han Chinese tourist families home with the idea that they've reconnected with *real* China.

Chinese conspiracy theorists and romantics alike consider the Hakka some kind of Chinese Illuminati because leaders and revolutionaries like Sun Yat-sen, Deng Xiaoping, and Lee Teng-hui all had Hakka blood in the veins. Are they the Chinese Masons? Are they the "Chinese Jews," as many people refer to them? Nobody knows for sure where Hakka people come from, why they emigrated to southern China, or what the exact racial distinctions between Hakka and Han Chinese are, but both sides want you to know that somewhere, someway, somehow these very important distinctions exist.

The handling of Hakka identity in China constantly reminds me that *whiteness* is everywhere. Something oppressive rises to the top in every country and inevitably declares itself the cream. You may call it aioli and he may call it Kewpie, but rest assured there are white people everywhere, and they gonna want mayonnaise on their wedding shrimp.*

Hakka Heather's entire business was based on attracting the gaze of mayonnaise eaters worldwide. This is an excerpt from her website boasting "Hakka Lineage":

> On Chengdu's East Side reside a community of Hakka people whose ancestral lineage precedes the Ming and Qing dynasties — over 500 years ago. This enclave descends from generations more recently from Guangdong Province.

It goes on for another two paragraphs documenting the "rich spirit of unity and strong endeavors" inherent in Hakka culture. The website also made it clear who Hakka Homes was for:

> Hakka Homes provides housing for all sorts of travelers and visitors that find themselves in Chengdu. Whether you're from Poland or Peru, a student or an employee of a multi-national, we have rooms that are comfortable and affordable.

It reminded me of Popeye's "Annie, the Chicken Queen," or Ken Jeong in *The Hangover*—perpetuating the fantastical mysticism of their respective races for the enchantment of weary international travelers. But I had to give it to her: the highlighting of Polish-Peruvian students or employees of multinationals was some pretty specific and intriguing writing. If Hakka Homes didn't work out, Hakka Heather clearly had a future as a copywriter.

She greeted Evan and me with my least favorite question.
"So, you like the hip-hop?"

---

* The only time you will see mayonnaise at a Chinese dinner is Cantonese wedding shrimp.

"Yeah, I listen to hip-hop."

"Cool. Me, too. Hakka Bar play hip-hop."

"Word."

"I see your show. I think many people watch your show. My friend from Thailand is chef, he watch your show, too."

"That's cool!"

"I can't wait to try your food. I hear from Vice people you are great chef."

"I'm OK. I'm known for making sandwiches."

"Oh, I love sandwiches. What sandwich do you want to make?"

"I don't want to make sandwiches here. I want to cook things I eat at home and see what people think."

"Just home food?"

"Yeah, red-cooked pork, bitter melon, seaweed, tea eggs, homestyle food."

"Ahhh . . . why?"

"I'm just curious if people will like my food. I'm Chinese, but I grew up in America. What if I'm a fraud? Or maybe I'm not? I just always wanted to know what would be if I was born in China." I felt flop sweat forming on my forehead.

"Just make it spicy. People in Chengdu like spicy."

When people speak about regional palates, they always make it sound that simple. Every cuisine has a few go-to moves when you wanna preach to the choir. Paris'll put you to bed with butter and burgundy; Houston'll drip it up in au jus and drape it out with horseradish;* and Chengdu'll set your mouth on fire, then extinguish it with Newport guts.† And it's true, when you're lazy on a Sunday afternoon playing the matinee home game, you might roast a chicken on cruise control and hit it with regional bottled sauce, but this was my first time in Chengdu,

---

* HANH, you see what I did there. My favorite verse about Houston's is Jeezy: "While y'all robbin' and boostin', I'm standin' over the stove like I'm the chef at Houston's." #Snowman

† The first time I smoked a Newport, it felt like eating Sichuan peppercorns.

and I wasn't about to half-step and burn their palates before I understood them.

Upstairs from Hakka Homes, Heather ran two more spots: the Hakka Bar and the Living Room at the top of the Super 8. It was one of the main reasons Evan chose to stay at Hakka Homes. He had worked out an arrangement with Hakka Heather where we could cook at Hakka Bar on Friday nights and serve locals. The kitchen at Hakka Bar consisted of a sink, a cupboard, a fridge, and one jet burner. In every Chengdu home I visited, there was one very powerful burner that could power a wok. If you put a skillet over it, the flame would pour over the sides and roast your handle. It was great for woks, bringing water to a boil, and freebasing.

At the Living Room, Hakka Heather served "Italian" food cooked by an Irish guy who was dating one of her friends.

"You like Italian food?" she asked me.

"Yeah, my dad had an Italian restaurant and my girl is Italian."

"Ohhh, you should cook Italian!"

"I'm down to cook Italian, but I really want to cook Chinese and see what the locals think."

"No, no, no, locals will like your Italian! Authentic!"

"I mean, I know a few dishes, but I'm not an expert on Italian food. I'd rather cook Chinese."

"But we rather eat Italian! We have so much Chinese. Italian is so cool!"

"I want to know what Chinese people think about my Chinese food, not my meatballs."

"But you know the Italian! We rarely see Italians."

"You know I'm not Italian, right? I am Taiwanese-Chinese from America."

She looked at me quizzically. As if I just blew open her universe.

"But Americans make Italian food, no?"

"Yeah, we have a bastardized red-sauce version of Italian food and identity proliferated by Republicans from Staten Island, New Jersey, and parts of Pennsylvania, who would still love to call black people *mulignans* but have been told not to."

"But one day, you make this Italian?"

"Maybe."

She was disappointed with me. Being the flirty, bohemian Hakka representer she was, I'm sure she met a lot of foreigners who were quick to act the part and satisfy her curiosity. I didn't blame her. The eagerness to understand identity in listicles and soundbites wasn't specific to Hakka Heather; she couldn't be the only one reading Buzzfeed, right?

But I decided to hold back and resist her invitation to speak in broad strokes about American demographics. Usually, I enjoyed exporting my gross caricatures of American whiteness for comedy, but a little bit of knowledge can be dangerous . . . especially in eager hands, without a radar for sarcasm, like Hakka Heather's. While Evan just feigned ignorance of the things Hakka Heather asked about, I just kept asking "Why?"

Why do you like Italian? Why do you like America? Why are you sick of China? And then we started to get somewhere. I looked around—despite her anywhere-but-here approach to Chengdu, Hakka Heather was too impressive to dismiss. Still in her late twenties,* Heather had a one-floor boutique hotel brand, a hip-hop bar, and an Italian restaurant. She'd done well for herself and clearly understood her habitat. I wanted to know how she did it.

"Yo, Heather, how'd you get into this business?"

"When I young, I party. I meet people. I start business."

Veni, vidi, vici.

"So you partied, you met people, and you opened up a hotel within a hotel?"

"Yeah, then I open bar and restaurant."

Anticipating my skepticism, Evan jumped in: "Dude, Heather knows everyone. I came to Hakka Bar one night, you could buy anything: hats, bootleg Pyrex, weed, hash, tickets to a party at Jellyfish. Everyone meets here at night."

"You party, you meet people, you open business. You don't open business, you lose."

---

* I didn't want to ask Heather her age, but I was told she was twenty-seven.

"You ain't lie."

"No, I don't lie. I tell you truth in China. YOU MUST DO THE BUSINESS! My parents lose their business, then they lose their home, then the government move them to new area. Many Chinese, the government want their property, they take it, then move them. Life not fair. Also, I own business, I wake up when I want to wake up. I sleep when I want to sleep. I party when I party and make money when I party. YOU MUST DO THE BUSINESS IN CHINA."

I let it soak in. It was one of the most frantic yet clear-eyed pleas for kill-or-be-killed commerce in China I'd ever heard. Not only that, it was generous—anytime someone speaks the truth when they could've just deflected, it's a gift. Hakka Heather gave me one and then offered up another.

"So you want to try real Chengdu food?"

"Yeah, what's good?"

"My brother has a restaurant that's very good. You can learn from him."

"What's the spot called?"

"Wei Ji Rou."

"Cool, what kind of food?"

"*Wei ji rou.*"

No hesitation, no apologies, your mans does one thing: spicy cold chicken.

Hakka Heather, Evan, and myself got in a cab and rode toward her brother's spot.

"Yo. Heather, why's the internet so slow at Hakka Homes?"

"Not Hakka, internet slow everywhere in China."

"Well, I know it's blocked, but it's slow even on unblocked sites."

"Yes, I know. Slow on purpose. China doesn't want us use internet."

"Stop playin'."

"Yeah, Ed," Evan interjected. "I talked to the Beijing Vice dudes, they said it takes a full day to upload a five-minute video."

"China keep us blocked out. We can't see anything without VPN."

"What's VPN?"

"VPN give you IP address in different country so you can see the internet."

"I mean, you can see the internet, it's just slow."

"No, with VPN you can read *New York Times*, Google, Twitter, Facebook. We can't even Facebook in China!"

"Trust, it's better without Facebook."

"Easy for you to say, you already had it."*

We drove another ten minutes, construction sites everywhere we went. China was disappearing by the second. Scooters weaved around the trucks and construction barriers, out of the past and into the present. Some scooters had half a hog on the back; another with whole chickens laid across the rear hopped a curb to make an illegal left turn.

It started to rain. At a stoplight, I saw a guy with a wheelbarrow full of wood put plastic bags on his feet, then buck across the street. There was no mercy. As soon as the light turned green, wheelbarrow man didn't trip, he knew what time it was. All is fair on a Chinese six-lane thruway.

"Damn, that dude almost got hit."

"Chengdu too fast now."

"People can stop, though."

"Selfish. Everybody think somebody else will stop, so they keep going."

"That don't make sense. It only works if everybody stops."

"Yeah, well, I stop but nobody else stop, still no use."

We finally got to the restaurant. It was in a nice part of Chengdu, once we got off the thruway. There was a sidewalk, preppy Chinese women in tennis skirts, dudes on beach cruisers, and a G-Wagon in the parking lot. Inside the restaurant, there were a few large parties.

I couldn't tell who had the G-Wagon. It's a fun game to play in China. Whose G-Wagon is it anyway? You can never tell who's the real stunna in China. First of all, there's a lot that's counterfeit. Some people are also hood rich. But people who really got dough may come through with a visor, shorts, tank top, and dress shoes, then drive home in a G-Wagon. Chinese people just don't care. I'd see what I thought was a lunch lady

---

* "Popular Demand" . . . Pusha T.

roll through with a Chloé bag, order three dishes, and return two 'cause they were cold.

On a table catty-corner to us, I saw the spicy cold chicken. I hit the punching bag in my mind, it smelled so good.

"That is *wei ji rou*."

It was a real humble-looking dish to the virgin eye, just hacked-up bits of brown bone-in chicken.

"*Wei ji rou* look simple, but very special. My brother ate this dish at restaurant once, then beg the chef to teach him for long time. He buy the recipe and practice, make his own change, then open *wei ji rou* restaurant."

I checked the dish on other people's plates and noticed the caramel color, the bouncy skin, the sharp edges on every cut. Each piece looked like chicken sushi, little Lego bits of brown chicken with the bone hanging by a thread. Finally, our *wei ji rou* arrived. It was spicy, it was tingly, it was grounded by the leeks, but listen. . . . I know you ninjas fuck with cold pizza so peep game. There is a particular sweetness that comes from the essence of cold poultry captured and frozen in time. Serving chicken cold isn't some lazy, check-what-I-made-last-night shit. There are certain dishes that channel the properties of a cold bird and capture a sweetness that echoes in your mouth, like you are chomping on cold chicken chewing gum with Sichuan peppercorns. Yes, that sounds fucking disgusting, but if Altoids dropped Spicy Cold Chicken Mints, you could open a tin over John Doe's face and give a cadaver a boner, that's how good the shit was. And that's why distilling a regional palate to modifiers like "it's spicy" doesn't work; it's deeper than that.

Everything else at his restaurant was hot trash. Literally, steaming hot trash. They brought out a plate of steamed green beans and squash with chili sauce to dip it in. Illest Chinese Struggle Plate I'd ever seen. Limp green beans and squash sentenced to death in mediocre chili sauce. But unless you're a Yelper, it really doesn't matter if they have ninety-nine problematic dishes, it's a Sam Perkins* restaurant.

---

* The god Sam Perkins can't do shit but shoot flat-footed threes, but it's enough.

I sat there and marinated on the *wei ji rou*. I laughed to myself 'cause I used to hate these brown chicken dishes, where you spent most of your time gnawing on bones. It was my grandma's *Dong'an ji*, a classic Huna-nese dish, that schooled me on the genre. Grandma Huang stayed with us in Orlando for a while, and every few weeks she'd buy some dark meat, chop it up, stir-fry it with chilis, garlic, wood ear fungus, bamboo, green onions, dark soy, and wine and fuck the spot up. I remember it stunk so bad my brand-new Penny Air Ups smelled like Dong'an chicken after she made it. And for what? I looked at this bowl of jagged chicken bones with small pieces of brown meat and wood ear fungus popping up like hemorrhoids. Twelve-year-old Eddie hated Dong'an chicken.

"Mom, these bones in the chicken just make me feel poor!"

"What? Bone-in chicken make you feel good! Nutrition in the bones."

"Nutrition in the bones. Nutrition in the skin. Nutrition in the carti-lage. I feel poor from all this nutrition."

"Where you think chicken meat comes from? The bone! You want to pay more money so somebody hide the bone from you?"

"Yeah, I don't want to see it! I don't want the blood from the bone, I don't want to spit the bits out, why can't you just buy tenders?"

"*HUANG SHOO SIN! NI ZU GHU ER ZHI FA FONG LU!*"*

Pops ran downstairs like someone broke in the crib.

"What happened? What's going on?"

"Your son too good for the chicken bones now! He want chicken tenders!"

"Chicken tenders twenty-three cents more per pound than bone-in breast and sixty-nine more than boneless skinless thighs and a dollar seven more than chicken quarters! Chicken tender is like Hennessy X.O."

"You think we have money for Hennessy X.O.?"

"Dad just bought a Dodge Stealth! Why can't we eat chicken ten-ders?"

"Dodge Stealth! Dodge Stealth? My Dodge Stealth cheaper than Mitsubishi 3000 GT! That is VALUE sportscar."

---

*   "LOUIS, YOUR SON HAS LOST HIS DAMN MIND!"

"There is no such thing value sportscar! You buy that car so we can't ride with you!" screamed my mom.

"Don't make me look like bad guy. That car fits four people!"

"Yeah, and you have *five* people in your family, plus your mom: six! And that seat so small, you couldn't fit four Fukienese people!"

Fukienese people being known for packing dragon boats into New York.

"Look what you did! Now your mother going to yell at me all week because you stupid ass want Dong'an chicken tenders!"

"No such thing Dong'an chicken tender! You want Dong'an chicken tender, better wait till McDonald's figure out Hunan food!"

"Ha ha, yeah, fat-ass Eddie go to McDonald's for Dong'an chicken tender. . . . Hi, I'm Eddie Huuuuuang. My fat ass wants Dong'an chicken tenders with sweet and sour sauce please."

My pops loved imitating me, but I deserved it. I wanted chicken tenders because they were convenient, they were clean, they weren't challenging. Dong'an chicken was fiery, complex, flavorful, and inconvenient. Your breath stank, your hands got dirty, and you had the illest spicy farts when you played Mortal Kombat later that night. When I had Dong'an chicken every other week, I couldn't run from it fast enough. But then Grandma left. I remember my mom trying to make Dong'an chicken.

"*Ay-yah! Ni yoh jah lu chu!*"*

"Dong'an chicken too straightforward without vinegar, just dry heat and bamboo!"

"That is Hunan food: dry, sharp, heat! You made this chicken ceviche!"†

"I like vinegar! Spicy needs sugar and vinegar. You don't know food."

---

* "Ayyy, you added vinegar again!" complained my dad.

† Take note: my dad is constantly speaking in broken English, but make no mistake. Homie had an extremely wide base of food knowledge. He owned, by my count, eleven restaurants over the years: Atlantic Bay Seafood, Cattleman's Steakhouse, Fajita Grill, Shrimp 'n Brew, The Mill Bakery and Brewery, Cattleman's on I-Drive, Corleone's (LOL), Coco's Floribbean, Aussie's Steakhouse, Bola, and The Black Olive. Not bad for a knucklehead from Taipei.

"What are you talking about, I don't know food? My restaurants pay for this food!"

"Grandma's is better, Mom. Stop adding vinegar to everything."

*"Xiao Tsen, ni biao tsa jwa!"**

Once I got my driver's license, I got to eat all the chicken tenders I could stand. Barbecue, sweet 'n' sour, Polynesian, honey mustard, Tabasco ketchup, etc. I'd tried pretty much every chicken tender, and they were all the fucking same. Most of the time dry, sometimes tender, but even then flavorless. The same went for pork loin. I'd buy chicken tenders to cook myself, trying to replicate my grandma's Dong'an chicken 'cause I couldn't stand all the vinegar in my mom's food.

"Ha ha, look at Eddie making Dong'an chicken tenders!"

"Oh, we got a McDonald's in this house now? Let me try!"

"Shut up, Dad! You can only make one dish."

"Two dish! Fried rice AND Taiwanese *mei fun*."

"And leftover paradise!"† said Emery.

"Oh, shut up, leftover paradise is just for survival when your mom is gone."

I took a bite of the Dong'an chicken tenders still in the wok.

"How is it?" asked Emery.

"Go away!"

"Don't be a dickhead, dude. I'll fuck you up!" threatened Emery.

I felt bad. Emery was just being curious, but I was embarrassed. The Dong'an chicken tenders were so stupid. It came out looking like something meant for a Panda Express steam table. Beautiful, glistening pieces of genetically engineered chicken breast surrounded by brown sauce and oriental vegetables. Sure, it was the portrait of convenience and refinement, but without the bones, the sauce had no depth. The wood ear

---

* "Xiao Tsen, don't you try to butt into this conversation!" (Xiao Tsen is my second Chinese name.)

† When my mom was out of town, my dad would pour all the food she'd made for us and left in the fridge together into one "new" dish he called "leftover paradise." It was more like the Guantanamo Blue Plate.

fungus and bamboo were lonely without the chicken bones and skin that usually came with Hunanese brown chicken hemorrhoid stir-fry. There's nothing I could add to re-create or mimic the essence of chicken bones. I had to lose it to love it. It's a lesson I'm still learning.

"Heather, why are all the pieces of meat so small in China?"

"You think it is small?"

"Yeah, I mean, this whole dish of *wei ji rou* is probably less than one chicken quarter cut up into ten really small pieces."

"I don't know. This is just what we eat."

"I like it a lot, but it'd be better if the pieces of meat were bigger."

"Hmmm, I don't know. It's flavorful this way. Small piece, lot of bone, you suck the bone."

"I guess, but I'd rather just have more meat."

"Are you hungry?"

"Oh no, I'm full."

"Then why you keep complain?"

She was right.

"You think if you didn't grow up eating *wei ji rou* like this, you would like it?" I asked her.

"I don't know. This is just how it is, but that's why I travel a lot. I have many different friends. American friends, Europe friends, Thailand friends, they show me things. Only way to see world is to get out."

"I guess it's the same everywhere."

"Not really. In New York, you have so many different people, things to see. China changing, but still too much of the same and not enough of the old."

"How so?"

"China, Chengdu, it's not the same anymore. We used to have so many trees, they said Chengdu was like heaven. Clear sky you could see the sun all the way to heaven. Chengdu looked like it was in one line to heavens."

"Yeah, you go to Manhattan. Manhattan don't got trees! But you want China to stay the same and be all trees? It can't stay the same if you want other people here one day, too."

"No, I welcome them to China! I want them to come stay Hakka Homes!"

"Ha ha, but you can't just see them as customers and transients. If you want white, black, brown people to come then you are going to have to let them bring their culture, their food, their values as well."

"I mean like this. China building and changing, but everything they build is the same. It is all malls! Malls, malls, malls, everywhere malls and all the same stores. China try to impress new world, new customer, new people, but we not showing people *real* Chinese. Nobody want to see these malls! These malls not Chinese!"

"For real, I rode around the other day and saw three Chanel stores. In all of New York City, there's three Chanel stores. I went online, Shanghai has five Chanel stores!" said Evan.

"And it's OK to build *some* malls, but now it is all malls and no teahouse. All the old teahouse, small restaurants, and nature go away. China find one thing that make money and people like: *malls* and that's all they build. The things that make Chengdu special all gone."

I started to appreciate Hakka Heather. She reminded me of twelve-year-old Eddie with the Wu-Wear in Orlando, associating difference with righteousness. The feeling comes from an honest place: being born an outsider and learning to love it instead of lamenting. You hang onto difference and deviance, taking them on as your identity. Over time you evolve from insisting on your difference to understanding it. One day, maybe you don't even need it. That day just wasn't today. I couldn't navigate acceptance. I only knew difference—and I stayed my ass outside.

The next day, Heather took us for a walk behind the Super 8. She wanted to show us another side of Chengdu off the main streets. We walked about a quarter mile down a back street, hung a right past some stalls and small grocers. This part of the neighborhood still had trees; there weren't fast food franchises, and families lived there. Every family sold something. Underneath every apartment was a garage that housed

scooters, mopeds, and a business. Some sold wind-up toys, others functioned as hardware stores, some had produce, one dude cut hair, and
everyone wore sandals.

"This is like Chengdu used to be. Much more relax, family hang out,
lots of trees, not so fast and noisy."

We walked another half mile with more of the same. Tea spots and
family restaurants started to pop up. There was a breakfast spot on every
block that sold steamed buns, soy milk or peanut drink, and dumplings.
None really stood out, the quality was mediocre, but they functioned like
the coffee and bagel carts that served New York neighborhoods. It was a
humble street with some charm, and if I had seen it as a twenty-two-year-
old, I would have spent eighty pages proudly telling you how this is what
the rest of the world should be.

After a while we stopped in front of a storefront.

"This is rabbit restaurant," Heather announced.

This was the main event on Hakka Heather's tour of local Chengdu
foods. She knew that I wanted to understand Chengdu cuisine and took
her role as an ambassador very seriously. I appreciated it.

The rabbit restaurant was a big restaurant with a huge menu contain-
ing seventy or eighty dishes. To contrast with the *wei ji rou* restaurant and
its one primary dish, Hakka Heather chose the large menu, Shopsin's-like*
approach with the rabbit restaurant.

I let Heather handle the ordering. What people don't realize coming
from abroad is that Chinese food in China is constantly changing. I remember in the early '90s when you wouldn't leave a Sichuan joint without eating *ma po tofu*, oil braised fish, spicy intestine casserole, or smoked
pork belly with leeks. These days, those dishes are dusty. People fuck
with them, but they're akin to steak au poivre, tableside Dover sole, or
beef bourguignon. It'll always be in the DNA, but they keep it moving.
The difference between Heather's rabbit joint and some goofy Sichuan-

---

* Shopsin's is one of my favorite restaurants in New York. Wassup Zack and Kenny! It's
known for having a huge, eclectic, rotating menu with mildly offensive but always entertaining names.

inspired modern "Chinese" restaurant in America is that Heather's spot wasn't inspired by Chengdu for downtown New York.* Heather's spot is the evolution of a craft that retains the characteristics and values from the source recognizable in its modern form. It survived independent of foreign consumption and could tell a story all its own that tourists could choose to understand or keep walking by.

Heather copped a fish mint salad, tea-smoked ribs, stir-fried rabbit bits with fresh chilis, ginger, and of course the whole roasted and shredded rabbit. I didn't mind rabbit, but I usually ate it in French restaurants like Brasserie Ruhlmann that served it over pasta or in a casserole with all the little bones. Here, the rabbit bits were picked up in a wok with high heat, glossy chilis, and a bit of ginger to neutralize the game. The temperature and a bit of cornstarch gave it a sheen that locked in moisture while still providing a nice exterior. Like the French rabbit dishes I'd had, though, it was a temperamental dish that relied heavily on who was on the wok. Today, it was a revelation.

The next dish was tea-smoked ribs. For generations, tea-smoked duck has been a cornerstone of Sichuan cuisine, and this was the first time I saw the technique on a St. Louis rib outside the crib. A lot of Chinese Americans or inquisitive Chinese aunties have taken their technique to the St. Louis rib, but I was hyped to try it in a restaurant, and it didn't disappoint. I gripped one up and the rib had a 3M sheen on the exterior.† I took a bite, and it opened up like valet. It was tender but not flabby, toothsome but giving.

Then came the whole roasted rabbit—well, they insisted it was roasted, but I knew it had Spanx on. I took the skin, tapped it with a spoon, got up under, and the protein had the tightness that comes from a quick douse of hot oil or a body suit. It was a great move. It brought back a little mois-

---

* This sentence doesn't refer to Chinese-American restaurants. The original Chinese-American restaurants served a localized cuisine created by immigrants to satisfy American tastes. At least in that form, Chinese people made a living watering down the cuisine, and America got what it wanted. I celebrate Chinese-American food just like Tex-Mex or Red Sauce Italian because it's how our people came up.

† I told you 'bout that 3M on the Jordan V, remember? DANCIN'.

ture, broke it up for better mouthfeel, and gave it a thinly crispy exterior. It had the skin of Cantonese roast duck, the sweetness of rabbit, and the texture of pulled pork, with an exquisite chili oil over the top.

"You should try the head," said Heather.

I'd heard that rabbit head was a Chengdu favorite, so I dove in. It wasn't like other gag foods where you're eating for the shock value or to say you survived it, like snake's gall bladder. The meat on the head was delicious, like juicy, fibrous, oxtail meat that happened to be on a rabbit's face: Protein Pangaea. I broke open the skull and ate the brains, too.

"That might be the best thing I've had in China," Evan said, and I agreed.

It felt great to be in China with my brother. Getting learned on Chengdu, Hakka people, and rabbit heads in our native habitat. Something about it was the same, but different, as if the spirits circling me had been present all along but were suddenly visible. I felt accepted by Hakka Heather, I was comfortable in Chengdu, and I felt a connection and familiarity to everything I was seeing and eating even though it was all brand new. Like a girl you met in a bar who you took to your apartment and who one day will take you to Scranton, Pennsylvania, so you can see her at home, au naturel, maybe even on a toilet.

I went back to Hakka Homes and was ready to call my mom.

"HALLO!"

"Hey, Mom, how's it going?"

"SLAVING. Your dad never help. I am cleaning the whole house, mopping, washing dishes, making him food, never stops, never helps!" It always made me mad hearing about this, but I tried to hold it together. I couldn't get derailed today. There were truths to tell.

"Well, make him help! And if he doesn't help, leave it dirty, stay in a hotel, and come back when he helps," I said, giving her the same play to run I've been giving her since I was twelve.

"Ay-yah, you don't understand, Eddie. Not possible! This is just how your dad is, and I have to take care of him."

"Why do you have to take care of him? He's old enough to take care of himself."

"No, no, no, opposite. He is too old to take care of himself. He gets confused all the time now, ha ha. He never remember where anything is now."

"But you don't have to pick up after him and clean everything. You're not his gofer."

"Eddie, Mom just complain to you. It's OK. He is your dad. He did everything outside the house, so I do everything in it. This is the way things are. How are you?"

"I'm good, Mom. I'm really good."

"Oh? Really? What happen? You have good news? New show?"

"No, not a new show."

"Hmmm, good business? How is second book?"

"It's good. I haven't been writing, but I wanted to talk to you about something."

"Yeah, tell me! What is it?"

"You promise you won't be mad?"

"I cannot promise that. You need to tell me first."

"Mom, you have to promise to be fair. I will tell you, but don't be emotional."

"Eddie, I don't know what you are going to tell me, but I cannot guarantee anything. Just tell me!" My stomach was in knots. I couldn't even say it.

"Eddie. . . . What's wrong?"

"Nothing, Mom. I'm really happy."

"That's good! That's good! Mom is happy, but what's wrong? If you are happy, why can't you tell me?"

"I think you're going to be mad."

"OK, baby, Mom won't be mad. You tell me."

"Mom. . . ."

"Yes?"

"I want to marry Dena, Mom."

"OH MY GOD! OH MY GOD! BABY, YOU MISUNDERSTAND YOUR MOM!"

She started crying hysterically. I didn't know what to say.

"EDDIE! All of you in the family misunderstand me. Why you all think I will be mad? I am so happy for you. You find someone to be happy with, who you have life with, you make family with, what mom will be mad? If you love her, if you pick her, then I am happy for you! Eddie . . . don't misunderstand your mom. Your mom love you no matter what. No matter what, no matter what you do, Mom love you. You are from me. You come from me. You are part of me. I am part of you. You are your mom. I cannot hate myself! I always love you and now I love Dena. I am your mom!"

"You are not mad she is not Chinese?"

"No! So silly! Your dad Chinese, he the worst. Ha ha, no, I love your dad, but it doesn't matter. Who cares if not Chinese?"

I thought about it for a second and came to a very disturbing revelation.

"I care."

Emery

My earliest memories are from 1985. I don't have many memories before that year, but I remember 1985. I was excited. My mom was making me a friend.

"He's going to be more than a friend!" my mom said. "He is your brother."

"Is that the best friend you can have?" I asked.

"Absolutely! Brother is best friend you will ever have."

"But you fight with your brother all the time."

"Ay-yah, Eddie, you little monster. I can't hide anything from you."

Mom thought to herself for a second then explained it to me. "I love my family, but we are not the best example. It was hard for our generation. Some born in China, some in Taiwan, everyone come to America have to learn new things. Life was hard. But you and your brother have to stick together, OK?"

"OK."

"Promise?"

"Promise."

In the weeks leading up to the birth, I hung on every word she told me about brothers. She told me a story about two brothers having a harmless fight in the kitchen that spilled over to the basement. One brother tumbled down the stairs and hit his head on a nail. He died.

She kept telling me morbid stories about brothers fighting to the death in preparation for my brother Emery's arrival. It freaked me out, but I was still excited. I wanted a best friend.

Dad didn't say much about Emery, but that didn't surprise me. He was always working late and I was asleep by the time he got home. When I woke up, he was already going back to work.

"Why is Dad so mean, Mom?"

"Your dad is not mean. He is under a lot of stress. Business is not good."

"Is that why he yells at you?"

"Eddie! When me and Dad fight, don't pay attention."

"You guys are loud."

"So nosy! Next time you hear us fight, you go sleep, OK?"

I didn't understand my dad back then and therefore I didn't like him. But on March 7, 1985, everything changed. Emery was born.

Dad came home from the hospital and picked me up. I remember he was very stern.

"Eddie, let's go see your mom."

"Is Mom still at the hospital?"

"Yeah, she just had your brother."

"Oh, cool! What's he look like?"

"He's big. Nine pounds, ten ounces. Fat baby."

"Awesome! He's gonna be tall!"

"Yeaaa, right!" He loved saying "yeaaa, right!"

We got in our Chevy Malibu station wagon and went off to the hospital. I didn't say anything to my dad. He didn't say anything to me. I just stared out the window at the trees. I liked the trees in Northern Virginia, passing now in a blur as we drove up and down the hills. It felt like we were on a roller coaster. Soon we pulled into the drugstore.

"I thought we were going to the hospital?"

"We need to make a stop here. Let's go."

"OK."

My dad walked into the store and I walked alongside him. He wasn't the kind of dad who would hold your hand or pat your head. He was more like a boss. I just followed his lead whenever he was around.

"Eddie, pick any toy you want."

"Really?"

"Yeah, but only one toy."

"What'd I do?"

"What do you mean?"

"Did I do something good?"

"No, not really."

I was suspicious. Was this a trap? My dad never did anything nice. Even my mom never got me toys. Something was wrong.

"Why am I getting a toy, then?"

He was hiding something from me. I remember he looked away and didn't make much eye contact.

"Eddie. Dad will always love you."

I didn't understand. He just kept staring at the wall of toys. If I was with my mom, I'd be bouncing off the wall picking through the toys, but I was careful around my dad. He always told me to walk straight, stand straight, chest out. I stood there as stiff as I could and stared at the wall with him. Then he spoke again.

"Xiao Wen,* your brother Emery is born today but I want you to re-member what I tell you. No matter what happens, no matter how much we love your brother, it doesn't change how we feel about you. Mom and Dad will always love you, OK? Nothing will ever change that."

"I know."

"How do you know?"

I shrugged.

"Really? You aren't worried that we may like Emery more?"

"No. I never thought about it. Emery is supposed to be my best friend."

"Ha ha, who told you that?"

"Mom."

"Hmmm, she's right. You have a good mom. I didn't know she al-ready told you this."

"Yeah, I wanna go meet Emery."

---

* My Chinese name was changed three times by a fortune teller. First it was Xiao Wen, then Xiao Tsen, then Xiao Ming.

"OK, well, pick a toy and then we go see Emery."

I knew exactly which toy I wanted.

"Dad, I want the green He-Man car."

But there was one problem with that choice. Just as my dad went to grab it, I spoke up.

"But I don't have a He-Man, Dad."

He wasn't falling for it.

"You want the car or you want a He-Man?"

"I want the car."

"You sure? This is what Americans call put the car before the He-Man."

"Yeah, I want the car."

"Why do you want the car?"

"The car is green. I like green. Plus, it's bigger. He-Man is just . . . a man."

"Ha ha, OK, here's your car."

He handed me the car.

Thirty-two years later, it's still here: the green He-Man car driven by a belief in unconditional love between father and son. Despite everything that's happened between us, I see myself as privileged. My dad stopped the world on March 7, 1985, to remind me that he loved me, and I'll never forget it.

I told myself that I'd take care of Emery the same way my dad took care of me. And in a way, I succeeded—I do treat Emery like Dad treated me: lots of cutting jokes and cheap shots sprinkled with random acts of kindness.

Emery hadn't been planning on coming to Chengdu, because he was eight chapters away from finishing a fantasy novel he'd been working on for two years. Most of the time he wouldn't even pick up the phone, 'cause he was in the lab. But China was something he couldn't resist.

I visited China because I knew it was good for me. Like eating broccoli. If you roasted the garlic just right, got that Maldon flake salt poppin', and kept the stems to a minimum, I might sit in an airplane for it. Emery, on the other hand, lived on frozen broccoli. Son kept bags of it in the freezer at home, microwaved it, and ate it like clockwork. I appreciated broccoli and China because I sensed they were good for me. Emery lived for them.

I shared a Netflix account with Emery, and every time I logged on, it was halfway through a Chinese, Korean, or Japanese film. Dude didn't watch anything in English besides *Braveheart*. He preferred Asian women, read *Asia Times Online*, couldn't wait for the rise of China—but, surprisingly, didn't care much about Chinese food. I asked him about it one time.

"I'm very allergic to MSG."

"You can be allergic to MSG?"

"Oh yeah, I get horrible headaches, dry mouth. I hate Chinese food in China."

Emery was one of the few people who went to China in spite of the food. He read so much news about recycled oil, fake meat, and exotic roach strains that it was impossible for him to eat Chinese food in China without imagining himself infected with some futuristic zombie virus.

"Why do you want me to come to China, though?"

"I need you to bring Mom's ring."

"Ahhh. You could just have her mail it, though."

I didn't want to get all sentimental on the phone, but it meant a lot to me that Evan and Emery would be with me in China when I proposed. But I couldn't just tell Emery. Like my dad, I offered a gift in place of communicating real human emotions and just hoped that he'd connect the dots on my design and understand why he had to be there. I mean, why actually tell someone how important he or she is to you when you can just offer airline tickets instead?

"Just bring it to China and I'll pay your airfare."

"That's it?"

"Yup . . . and help me cook."

"Hmmm. How much cooking?" Emery was always careful about committing to any work not involving a computer and headset.

"Just help out when we do events upstairs on the roof. I'll do the cooking, just help set up and serve."

"You sure?"

"I'm sure."

"I don't have to run payroll, go to the Liquor Authority, or get sued for a Four Loko party? You're not going to hotbox the basement and hang out with birds when Sam Sifton shows up?"

"Dick. Just set up and serve."

"If you ask me to help with the tax audit, I'm going to be very upset."

"Evan's on the tax audit."

"You know Evan is going to fuck up the tax audit."

"Motherfucker, just get on the plane. This is not a business deal. There are no hidden strings. I just want you to be out here for an important life moment 'cause you're my brother."

"OK, but every time I get excited for one of your life moments, you fuck your life up and then I try to fight you and you end up running around the apartment complex naked. I'm just trying to avoid seeing your balls again."

Every two years, Emery and I used to have an all-out, no-holds-barred fight. The last time we fought was in the parking lot of Cattleman's Steakhouse, right before my dad sold it. Emery was criticizing Evan's management of Baohaus, and I jumped in to defend Evan. Not because I didn't think Evan could improve, but because Evan was my mans, and if anyone was going to criticize my mans, it was gonna be me.

Emery was three years younger than me but had been stronger since eleventh grade; from that day on I stopped fighting him toe to toe and instead I'd Mayweather him. Stick and move and if all else failed, fight dirty. When he stepped to me in the parking lot, fists up, I ran into the adjacent construction site and found a rock. I threw the big-ass rock at Emery's stomach, stopped him in his path, and started beating him over the head with a wooden door stopper until Pops broke it up.

"You fight dirty!" Emery yelled once Dad pulled us apart.

"I didn't want to fight at all! You fucking started it."

"You run like a bitch."

"I don't want to fight, but if you're going to unilaterally decide that we're going to fight, I'm going to Mayweather you."

"Mayweather doesn't throw rocks and hit people with door stoppers, you fat fuck."

"He should. It'd be a lot more interesting."

Despite it all, Emery was my heart. While we argued the most, we had the same intentions and values. It's how we acted on those intentions and values that became the problem.

Three days after our phone conversation, Emery showed up at Hakka Heather's, exploding with excitement.

"Dude! This is a hooker hotel!"

"Ha ha, we picked a good one," said Evan.

"And it's next to a Hooters!"

"Yeah, man, they got broccoli and protein," I said.

"Oh, don't worry, I brought a case of Quest Bars from home. China is not going to ruin my digestive system this time. I refuse to shit my pants this trip."

"Good luck, my ass just randomly makes espresso with no warning out here and then I have to take a shower."

"UGH! No, no, Edwyn, I'm not shitting my pants this time. I refuse! This setup is too good for me to be sitting in this room shitting my pants. Do you realize where we are?"

"Starbucks?" Evan said. He'd seen too many off-menu espressos.

"No, dude, a CHINESE SUPER 8 HOOKER MOTEL. I can't wait to watch these round eyes walk in and out with hookers. This is the best trolling position ever! And yo, did you know there is an insurance company set up in the room next to yours? I just saw this delivery guy go up the elevator on a moped, ride it through the hall, deliver food to the insurance company, then drive back into the elevator and go downstairs."

Emery was right. China, at this moment, was a beautiful place. Especially if you believe heaven is a movie directed by the Coen Brothers.

"If you wanna see some ratchet shit, go to the meat market. I need some pork belly anyway," I said.

I was prepping all morning for our first event at Hakka Bar upstairs. The menu was something simple and familiar: red-cooked pork belly, seaweed knots, braised egg, bitter melon, and garlic cabbage. I live for the meat and three: rice, meat, three vegetables, and something sweet. It's a deal cooks have negotiated with the People since before I can remember. What does everyone want Sunday, Monday, Tuesday, and Wednesday once they move out of their parents' home? Mom's food. That's what the meat and three is: the ten-dollar reenactment of your mother's table. In this way, cooks are surrogate moms. Eating your way through the box, staring at the bottom of a greasy Styrofoam container, you come to grips with the distance between the already passing satisfaction and the memories it evoked. This isn't your mom's food; this isn't your mom's house; and this isn't your mom's love. It's a moment you bought for ten dollars: three songs about Mom at Karaoke Boho.

"Hakka Heather told me there are two meat markets. One in the mall and the other is what she calls the 'ultra premium' meat market," I told Emery.

"Oh, for sure, I'll go to the meat market. I bet it's so nasty. I'm going to finger swine rectum and make Evan smell it."

"Gross, dude! Don't fucking do that shit. I could get foot and mouth disease, man," Evan said.

Emery could smell blood in the water. He immediately picked his nose and chased Evan around the room with a stinky finger. I can honestly say with no irony, I really missed having Emery and his stinky finger around.

Evan and Emery decided to go to the Ultra Premium Chengdu Meat Market, so I went to Treat, the grocery store in the mall. I asked the locals in the lobby about whether I should walk or cab and got differing opinions.

"You could walk, but you will sweat."

"Hmmm, there is no train stop here."

"Must take cab, you will sweat."

"Must take cab, you will become dark."

Despite everyone's concern for perspiration and tanning, I got on my

N.Y. shit and walked. Chengdu has a subway system on par with, say, Philadelphia. You can walk a half-mile to any train station and go to most parts of the city. But in Chengdu, it's also possible to step outside and walk to your choice of three different super malls within a mile radius of your home; it's just not an enjoyable walk. There's nothing intimate or charming about it. Scooters, mopeds, and bikes zip around, cars jump the curb; at every turn there are six-lane streets, skywalks, and freeways. It's like some sort of ugly, twisted Ayn Rand nightmare: Architects Gone Wild.

If you've never been to a major Chinese or Russian city, it's tough to grasp how uncomfortable cities built by communists are. Just imagine if Redman and Mumm-Ra* collaborated on a city; that's what Chengdu looks like. A disgusting mummy lair accented with a touch of pre–Cory Booker Newark, neatly encased in a delicious cocoon of coal smog. You'll get robbed in West Philly, but it happens in a setting with spectacular Victorian architecture, and you're consoled knowing your hard-earned money is going toward a crispy pair of Air Force 1s or Meek Mill's funeral.† I'd rather be robbed in West Philly than massaged in Chengdu with a room facing the street; the views are so spectacularly putrid that it makes West Philly feel like Queen Anne's world.

After about twenty minutes, I arrived at Raffles City: a four-level mall concept developed in Singapore and transplanted in Chengdu. It had a Din Tai Fung noodle shop, a movie theater, office space, and this light pavilion installation that looked like one giant piece of backlit Chex Mix. Treat, the Hong Kong grocery store, was on the basement level. Approximately seventy percent of the businesses in Raffles City were international, and the prices were higher than in most places around Chengdu.

You walked around and saw almost all Asian faces, but there were levels to this shit. Teenage kids with disposable income and designer

---

*   Bad guy mummy from *ThunderCats*.

†   "Is that a world tour or your girl's tour?" I once told a friend I'd never quote Drake but . . . anything goes in the footnotes.

clothes politicked at the custard or red bean drink spots. Taiwanese restaurants and stands were popular with these kids because the food was
cheap. There were also Westerners with very idiosyncratic tastes. You
could never peg what a Westerner was going to try. Some were adventur-
ous, walking back to their office through the mall with pig ear on a stick,
while others played it safe with fried rice steamed in lotus leaves. The
older Chinese businessmen had an affinity for Gan Guo,* a popular Sichuanese dish featuring dry heat, aromatics, and your choice of protein
stir-fried and delivered to your table in a wok, the Chinese equivalent to
pasta-in-the-pan.

I'd become numb to malls. I'd grown up in mall-infested central Florida and had now seen malls on six of the seven continents. They were all
the same, phallic, egotistical structures with minor design distinctions; a
collection of broad-stroke stimulation under one roof aiming to please
everyone but really just leaving behind a lot of broken hearts and dirty
napkins in the food court. I was pondering the numbness when my
phone rang.

"Dude . . . did you just get my text?"

"No, I'm distracted. This mall is fucking horrible."

"Look at your phone, Edwyn."

It was Emery. I put him on speaker and opened up his text, which
contained three images. The first photo was a line of three stalls at the
meat market where a Chinese kid about six years old had pulled his
pants down and was pissing in the gap between a chicken and pork vendor.

"OK, so don't get any pork that kid pissed on."

"Keep looking, Edwyn. . . . I found the MOST ULTRA PREMIUM
CHENGDU MEAT."

I went to the second photo: black chickens and yellow chickens hanging from their necks over a giant rectangular butcher's block where huge
duck and chicken carcasses were laid out. Right in the middle of the
photo was a sleeping Chinaman.

---

*   Dry wok.

"Did you see it?"

"Son! This Chinaman is SLEEPING with a squad of dead chickens!"

"For real! It's the best! This meat market is fucking crazy. It smells HORRID, but there is so much ratchet shit going on. They are selling meat from this stand, and people are picking meat AROUND a sleeping Chinaman."

"I don't even want to see the third photo."

"Oh, the sleeper is my favorite, but I saved this one for last 'cause I know you'll be VERY impressed."

"Stop it. What is the third photo?"

"I can't tell you, Edwyn, it's too good. You need to see photo three for yourself."

Fuck it. I opened the third photo. Everything seemed OK, and it made me nervous. What the fuck did Emery want me to see?

"Do you see it?"

"Shut up, man, I'm trying to concentrate."

"OK, OK, let it sink in."

It was a stall with poultry and livestock hanging from hooks. I looked more closely at the animals: there was a black free-range chicken, a duck, a duck, a rabbit. No big deal. Wait a minute. . . .

"Emery . . . that's not a fucking rabbit."

"Ha ha ha, no, Edwyn. Rabbits don't have tails like that."

"THEY ARE SELLING FRESH DOG IN THIS MARKET?"

"Dude . . . DOG. I found fucking DOG. Now don't go telling all the white people you know! They're going to think we all eat dog."

That was the deadest-ass dog I'd ever seen in my life. The skin was tense, muscles taught, tail erect, head and neck still attached so you saw its face.

I made myself look at the image for a good five minutes.

In sixth grade, I wanted a dog.

"If you get straight A's, you can have a dog," my mother told me.

"What if I have an A minus? I have A's in five classes, but A minus in one."

"A is A. We are not monster parents. A minus is still A."

"Can I get a big dog?"

"How big?"

"I want a German Shepherd!"

My mom got a little misty.

"What? You don't like German Shepherds, Mom?"

"No! You always misunderstand me, Xiao Tsen. I love German Shepherd. I had one in Taiwan."

"Is it dead?"

"You so silly! Of course it's dead. Dogs don't live that long. You want dog, one day will die. I tell you. When I was in middle school, my dad had many dogs guard the textile factory. Lots of dogs. I love dogs. My favorite was a German Shepherd. Every day, I comb his hair, take him for walk, give him food. He was my best friend.

"I didn't have many friend. People all liars. This boy in school tell me he like me, but very annoying. Every day, he come chase me after school so one day I slam door behind me and his thumb get stuck. He don't like me anymore."

"But you slammed his thumb in the door."

"I didn't mean to slam his thumb in door. He stupid chase me too close! But if he really like me, he would try harder."

"Is this how all girls think?"

"Yeah, girls don't have many friends in life. Your dad sometimes not even my friend. But this German Shepherd was my best friend. So pretty, every day, hang out with me, follow me, and very kind. Life in Taiwan was hard back then, though. Lots of homeless people in the street. I never forgive myself. . . .

"One day, I say, 'I should let this dog run! I am not fast enough to keep up.' So I let the dog off the leash and run. At first he stay with me, he don't run. But I tell him, 'Go, go, you're free! Go run!' So he run.

"I wait for him. Ten minutes, he no come back. Twenty minutes, no dog. Thirty minutes, I start to walk around look for my dog. I'm so nervous. Searching, searching, 'Where is my dog?' Then I find him and I cry. I cry, I cry, I cry. The homeless people in Taiwan have metal hooks on rope. One of the homeless hooked my dog leg and pull the meat off. Dog get away, but limping back to me with part of leg missing. Make me so mad! These people are sick! Sick people, who would do this to dog? I so mad at myself and everyone. Only friend I have, they take his leg. . . ."

My mind scrambled and I felt something like shame when my mother told me this story. I thought, Wait, so not only do "our people" eat dog, but they line catch the leg and that leg came from my mother's dog?

These days, I realize my shame was misplaced. When I think about that dog now, I feel sadness, but not any specific pain for being Chinese-Taiwanese because that has nothing to do with it. I thought about what Emery said, *Now don't go telling all the white people you know*, but why not? If someone is poor enough to fishhook their neighbor's dog for a meal, it's on us to figure out why someone in this corner of the world consciously makes that choice. Being Chinese doesn't instantly give you a thirst for dog fishing, but getting left behind will give you a hunger for anything that moves.

"Ed, we're gonna come meet you back at Hakka Homes. I don't think you want any of the pork at this meat market," Emery broke into the silence.

I ended up getting all of my ingredients at the thoroughly air-conditioned super mall.

I got back to the crib, cut the pork belly, flash boiled it, and red-cooked it like we do at Baohaus, except I replaced the Wild Cherry Pepsi we use there with seaweed. Like going Côtes-du-Rhône instead of Beaujolais, trading ripe fruit for an earthy bass line. I paired the pork belly with stir-fried cabbage using a hint of dry chili, vinegar, light soy, sugar, and garlic. Similar to Jamaican stewed cabbage but sharper and fresher, like draft sake.* The cabbage was something I wanted people to mix, mash, and throw alongside everything. Eating at potlucks, I'd always nab a piece of

---

* *Nama,* or draft sake, is unpasteurized. It's my favorite. You get more floral notes; it's fresh and very springtime.

pork, marry it to some cabbage, then shovel a grip of rice into my mouth with pork jus to wash it all down.

Meanwhile, I sliced the bitter melon, chopped fresh chilis, grated some ginger, and set up the rest of my place.*

I was trying something new with the bitter melon. Usually, people would just *gan tsao*—"dry cook"—the bitter melon with some salt and oil and embrace the bitter cooling effect. Bitter melon is one of the seminal ingredients in Sichuanese cooking because it neutralizes heat. When you eat a spicy, numbing dish, it just makes sense to eat something cool and bitter alongside it.

I wanted to use a Sichuanese ingredient but prepare it in a Taiwanese way. So, I did a *xiao tsao:* "little stir-fry." Like *lu wei, xiao tsao* is a classic technique where you could take any vegetable or even cured pressed tofu, stir-fry it with dried baby fish and peanuts, and serve it hot or cold. Moms loved it because you could make it and set it aside. I'd go play *Mike Tyson's Punch-Out!!* in the basement, walk up, take a few bites of *xiao tsao* over rice, and then run back downstairs. For me, cooking has always been about ideas and techniques, not recipes. *Xiao tsao, lu wei, hong sau,* these all began as ideas, then they became techniques and eventually one ingredient fit so well with the idea that it somehow usurped the idea: *hong sau* pork belly, *lu wei* duck wings, and stir-fried bitter melon are probably the best renditions of the ideas. But I think the great cooks remember the philosophical roots: *hong sau, lu wei,* stir-fry, g-funk, bounce, trap, triangle, motion, Princeton—to me it's about the idea. People and pork come and go, but ideas? Ideas can be bigger than all of us if we just let them grow.

I started by opening up the fresh chilis in the wok, then hit 'em with some grated ginger. Quickly, before anything browned, I added dried baby fish and peanuts, and tossed it over and over. You want all the ingredients glossy, shining with oil, but not dry or browned. Then came the

---

* Cooks say "mise-en-place" = everything in its place. Then you abbreviate it like, "Yo, Liam, you got your place ready?" Or, "J.R., you got the place packed?" You're asking if your homie has all the ingredients for the dish he's making ready, in their proper place, ready to cook. Like anything else, cooking is about preparation.

bitter melon, sugar, splash of vinegar, salt, white pepper, and at the last second, I saw a bottle of *wai jwa* (crooked mouth grain alcohol)* that I picked up from a street stall. Without really thinking too hard about it, I took a sip, then dashed it over the bitter melon.

FLAMES!

Literally, my wok flamed up, but I continued to toss the bitter melon until the flame went out. When the fire cleared, I looked down into the wok . . . no burns, no brown, just perfectly wok-tossed *xiao tsao*.

"Eddie, are you OK?" screamed Emery.

"Yeah, I'm fine, I just flambee'd some bitter melon."

"Stupid! You're cooking in a closet and breathing in carbon monoxide! OPEN THE DOOR!"

He was right. I was having such a good time in the kitchen with the high-BTU burner that I forgot I was literally trapped in the five-by-five closet that separated the balcony from the living room. The glass door to the living room was fogged up with grain alcohol vapors and chili fumes. I started to cough and wheeze as I leaned over to the door.

"Fucking China!"

"It's not China's fault you're hotboxing yourself with bitter melon in the kitchen closet."

"It is *definitely* China's fault that this kitchen is also a closet. Look, there are hooks for hanging laundry on the wall in front of the stove!"

When we first got to the apartment, there were actually towels and socks from the previous guests hanging from those hooks.

"Did you just burn grain alcohol?"

"Yeah, this *wai jwa*."

"In bitter melon?"

"Yeah, try it."

Emery skeptically dug in. Took a few nibbles, thought to himself, and spoke. "Interesting. It's weird and different, but good. Bitter, a little

---

* A brand of *bai jioh,* white liquor, sold in a bottle with an offset neck, so they call it crooked mouth *bai jioh.*

sour. . . . There's a lot going on. Bitter melon is usually pretty plain and bitter."

"Do you like it like that, though? The usual way gets boring."

"Yeah, I've never been a bitter melon fan, but people here fucking love that shit. I just don't know what they're going to think."

"Well, try the seaweed."

"You put seaweed in the pork?"

"Yeah, you like?"

"Mhhm, good. Smart. I like it more than the way Mom does it with five-spice. I get a headache from five-spice now."

"You get a headache from all Chinese food."

"That's why I don't eat Chinese food; food is utilitarian. It serves a functional purpose, and if it gives me a headache after I eat it, it fails that functional purpose."

"I want to enjoy my food! What's the point of living to a hundred if you eat frozen broccoli and chicken all day?"

"That's a hundred years I get to play RTS* games online and watch porn."

"Well, you have positive outlets. I need to die as soon as possible because any extra time I have I'll spend watching the Knicks."

Emery was the contrarian's contrarian. All through school, teachers thought I was crazy, an iconoclast without a cause. When Emery came around, all records were shattered. He was like Peyton Manning, laughing at bum-ass Wrangler-wearing Brett Favre's accomplishments and systematically flicking each record away.

If I characterized America as something with a lot of promise that had a very smelly belly button, Emery would say it was a valley of lepers and liars spreading the gospel of infectious disease across the seven seas. That it never had promise, that it had no intention of fostering democracy, freedom, or diversity, but instead was a strategic reaction to the supply-and-demand dynamics of the global political economy at the time. Of

---

*   Real-time strategy.

course, he'd bring up slavery, the slaughter of Native Americans, and the Chinese Exclusion Act as his best evidence. And he was right.

"BRRRZZZZ!"

My doorbell rang just as I was packing up the pork for our party at Hakka Bar. It was Evan.

"There are a bunch of people at Hakka Bar already, you ready?"

"Yup, start taking up the rice cooker, make ten cups of rice."

"OK, you want me to use the bottled water?"

"Definitely."

I chopped some fresh cilantro, washed the chopsticks and bowls, and started bringing things up to Hakka Bar.

I took the elevator up and walked across the balcony until I reached Hakka Bar, a former Super 8 Motel suite with a patio and door blown out. Hakka Bar was popular in the neighborhood and always had a solid group of customers, but Hakka Heather told all her friends that we were cooking that night, so the crowd was younger than usual. One homie who looked like a cannonball in a wife-beater walked up to me, spliff in mouth.

"HIP-HOOOP," he said in a sleepy Chengdu drawl.

"Ha ha, what up, hip-hop?" I responded.

Hakka Heather came over with another young woman—similar height, similar braid in the hair, similar bootleg green 59/50 hat with puffy Chinese writing on the dome.

"Eddie!" Heather greeted me. "Look! Hat says 'Hip-Hop.'"

I felt like I was staring at my boy's University of Michigan hip-hop T-shirt from 2002 and cried laughing inside. I was trying to figure out what was cornier: Ann Arbor business school stairwell hot 16s or Chengdu Super 8 Motel Rooftop cyphers. Quickly, I realized that Hakka Heather had promoted me to her friends as a hip-hop chef and felt transported back to a Food Network development meeting.

"These are my friends. They all like the hip-hop and want to try your food. Very excited to meet you."

"HIP HOOOP!" said the chubby Chinaman once again.

"What's your name?" I asked him in Mandarin.

"Huo Tse!" he said. Train.

"Word, how'd you get that name?"

"I work on the train."

"I like that. Utilitarian alias."

"What did you cook?"

"Hong sau pork, chili cabbage, bitter melon, seaweed. . . ."

"Ahhh, good taste. Twenty-five RMB right?"

"Yup, twenty-five RMB a plate."

Twenty-five RMB was about $3 U.S.—the same cost as a bowl of noodles and sliced pork from the vendors downstairs. Twenty-five RMB gets you a well-rounded meal on the street in China, even in Shanghai.

In the back of Hakka Bar, Evan had the rice cooker, butane burners, and chafing dishes ready in an apartment kitchen. I unloaded the pork belly into a wok set over the butane burner on low, the cabbage went in a chafing dish, and the bitter melon *xiao tsao* and seaweed went on large platters. I plugged in my iPod, played some Dipset, and got ready to serve. The people in the bar started to pick up plates and line up. Huo Tse was first. I put two scoops of rice on his plate, topped it with pork, au jus of red-cook, bitter melon on the side, seaweed, and cabbage in the front.

"EY! Can I get some more rice?"

"Yeah, no problem. You want more pork?"

"No, no, no, too generous. Just more rice."

"Huo Tse always hungry!" said Hakka Heather. Then she turned to me.

"You don't need to give more pork. For twenty-five RMB, you already giving way too much meat, just give rice if they are hungry."

Hakka Heather and the other people were policing the portions for me. I just wanted people to try my food, but Heather felt like they were already getting a deal and it was bad face for them to ask for more.

"Hey! I heard you are from Taiwan, too!" said a customer bum-rushing the serving table. He was darker than everyone else, had longer hair, and looked like some sort of Chinese surfer.

"My parents are overseas Chinese born in Taiwan, but I was born in America."

"Then you are Taiwanese like me! Look at your food, must be Taiwanese."

He got his plate, gave me 25 RMB, and walked his way down the line.

"This looks great," he said, "but you gotta peel the eggs for people. In Taiwan they would peel for you."

"You are not in Taiwan anymore!" said Hakka Heather and ushered him away to a booth.

Within minutes, everyone had assumed positions. Customers scoped the situation, Evan received the cash, Emery scooped rice onto plates, I loaded the meat and three, and Hakka Heather kept the line moving. Despite my third-grade Mandarin, no one tripped. The best part of serving simple homestyle food is that nothing gets lost in translation. If what you're doing is real, people will walk through walls for it and assume the position, a.k.a. the squat & shovel.*

The next customer was interesting. He had a Been Trill hat and Pyrex shorts on like a Chengdu clone of SoHo kids hanging on Lafayette Street. It was actually the first time I'd been to China outside Shanghai and seen someone rocking a current N.Y. style without any sort of mutation. He didn't finish the look with a fanny pack or white tube socks and a bowl cut.

"Wassup!" said the homie in relatively unbroken English.

"Sup. I'm Eddie."

"I am Xiao Li. Very excited to try this food. Heather tell us all about you."

"Word, well, I hope you like it, fam. It's just simple potluck food."

"Ha, you are the kidding. Red-cooked pork not so simple: Holiday Style."

---

* When Chinese people freestyle, they squat and eat. No matter where you are, no matter what you're wearing, Chinese people are seemingly just predisposed to squatting and shoveling food into their mouths with chopsticks. For purposes of urban development, I think this is a very futuristic maneuver.

Xiao Li was right. I'd become desensitized to the fact that Baohaus was in effect Taiwanese Boston Market,* serving a slice of Chinese New Year every day. Growing up, red-cooked pork was a holiday dish you'd eat for Grandma's birthday, Moon Festival, or Chinese New Year but we'd gotten so used to doing it every day at Baohaus I didn't associate it with Chinese New Year anymore.

I made him a plate. He nodded his thanks.

"If you want to smoke, we have the weeds outside."

"Word, I'll come thru."

"Also, what is this music you playing?"

"DIPSET!"

"Hmmm, what is Dipset?"

"What do you mean, 'What is Dipset?'"

"Like, what is this? I never heard."

"Motherfucker, Dipset is the greatest!"

"Hey, man, you cool, but why you call me motherfucker."

"It's just a way of saying 'you.' My bad."

"I don't think motherfucker means 'you.' You just called me person who fuck mother, how does this mean 'you'?"

"No, like, you MY motherfucker, you may not fuck other people's mothers or my mother, but you MY motherfucker."

"I know this word, but I don't know why I am your motherfucker."

"It's like sometimes people in Chinese say *lao sai*, or son of a bitch, but you still cool."

"Ohhh, OK, I understand but kind of don't understand. . . ."

We were mercifully interrupted by the Taiwanese homie.

"*WA SAI!*" screamed Taiwanese Point Break.

"Ha ha, it's good?"

"This five flower pork [pork belly] is great. Very tender and flavorful, spicier than most red-cooked pork and less sweet so I like it, but I have NEVER had anything like this seaweed, it's even better than pork!"

---

* Boston Market basically serves Thanksgiving every day.

"Thanks, man, it's easy. Just put the seaweed knot in the red-cook."

"I know, it's so simple, someone should have thought of it! But . . . you know what is my favorite?"

"What?"

"This *xiao tsao*! I see exactly what you did. TAIWANESE *XIAO TSAO* WITH BITTER MELON! Very funny interpretation, I like."

Just as I was about to thank him, a guy with stunna shades and a CDC snapback rolled up to the line, rockin' all Huf everything, alongside a friend who looked like a Fung Wah bus driver with lanyards on his neck and bookish glasses.

"What is this going on?" said Stunna.

"Twenty-five RMB, you get red-cooked pork, cabbage, seaweed, a braised egg, and bitter melon with rice."

"OK, OK, not bad deal. I want three. Two for me, one for my friend Fish, here."

He pointed to the Fung Wah bus driver.

"Cool, what's your name?"

"Rabbi."

The teacher of the Torah watched intently as I made the plates. Rice first, then pork, cabbage, seaweed, braised egg, and . . .

"What's that?"

"Bitter melon."

"I know bitter melon, but why you have fish in bitter melon?"

"I think it tastes good."

"I don't know. We don't eat bitter melon like this in Chengdu."

Point Break came to my rescue.

"Eh! *Da gu*, try it first! New style Taiwanese *xiao tsao*."

"Ahhh, this is Taiwanese food?" exclaimed Rabbi.

"I don't know, man. I'm *wai-sheng ren* born in America, so I'm not really sure."

"Ha ha, you funny man. What do you think it is?" laughed Rabbi.

"My dad told me as a kid, I'm Hunan, so you Hunan. I guess it's Hunan."

"OK then. Hunan in the house!"

Point Break got tight.

"No, no, no, that is definitely Taiwanese food. You are Hunan but cooking Taiwan style. *Xiao tsao* is for sure Taiwanese!"

"But the bitter melon must be Sichuan or Hunan," said Rabbi.

"We have bitter melon in Taiwan, too!"

"Yes, you have, but we famous for bitter melon. This is our dish."

"Sure, but Xiao Ming here apply Taiwan style, now we the more famous, ha ha ha!"

"Whatever man, I tell you after I try it." Rabbi settled.

I looked down at Rabbi's ankle.

"Fam . . . what is that on your ankle?"

Your mans had the most official 2001 Brooklyn summertime round-the-way-girl wrist tattoo on his ankle.

"Oh, you know this? FABOLOUS."

"Of course I know Fab, but why do you have a Fab tattoo on your ankle, homie?"

"I am hip-hop-head. First article I ever wrote was on Fabolous, so I tattoo on my ankle."

"Damn . . . what if your first article was on Spliff Star?"

"Then I might have Spliff Star tattoo."

"That's deep."

Rabbi walked away with his plate and continued to eye the bitter melon.

Emery sidled over.

"I don't like these hip-hop posers."

"What's wrong with you, man?"

"They're just consuming black culture without any connection to it. They live in Chengdu."

"Son, the culture is international."

"Well, you're blind to it sometimes, too. You grew up with it, but you're not black, either."

"Emery, it's not about being black. Nineties hip-hop is some civil disobedience shit. If homie tattooed Thoreau on his ankle, you wouldn't call him a poser."

"Thoreau's shit isn't tied to a racial struggle! Hip-hop is specific to the black experience."

"Yes, it came from a very specific experience, but it's transcendent *just* like Thoreau. You can't tie culture down to anything, you have to let it mutate and adapt and evolve."*

"I'm just sick of people in China always sucking on America's tit for inspiration when there's plenty to draw from here."

I understood Emery's frustration. Nobody likes posers. People in China literally rented white people to pose as experts, butlers, and models to provide a layer of "authority" or "excellence" to everything and anything in China. Emery despised this worship of whiteness because it took incredible strength to love his own skin. He wanted Chinese people to look within. People like Rabbi, Xiao Li, and myself struggle because whiteness is a universal problem, but luckily, intergalactic black culture is something we've seen ourselves in. While many people want us to treat black culture like an oasis we're passing in the larger cultural desert, I sat down in it because to a cottonmouthed traveler that's spent his life circling a cul-de-sac, water is just water.

Just as we were about to rip each other's faces off, Rabbi returned with Fish.

"Hey, man! This bitter melon is crazy! I've eaten bitter melon my whole life and never had this flavor. What did you do? So fresh."

"I just stir-fried it with vinegar and *wai jui bai jioh*."†

"Oh, wow. This is local *bai jioh*, but I never see anyone cook with it. Crazy. Sitting here in front of us whole time, but American Taiwanese come back and use it with bitter melon. . . . So crazy."

The bus driver spoke. He hadn't said a word all night, but you could

---

*   In the heat of the moment, I didn't have the space to qualify this against the backdrop of appropriation, but in retrospect, I didn't need to. Appropriation is when something is taken and ripped, then reapplied as a skin for a different definition and idea. What I'm talking about here is for the idea to remain intact but to mutate and evolve within itself in relation to the environment, without being plucked by the invisible hand. #FuckYouAdamSmith

†   Crooked mouth *bai jioh*.

see him intently studying the food wanting to understand everything going on in the plate.

"Uhhh, Eddie, right?" said Fish.

"Yeah!"

"OK, so, I was very excited to eat your food. I am *tse huo** and I very much pay attention to these things. Rabbi is right. This bitter melon is very special."

"Most special!" said Rabbi.

"Yes, but Rabbi likes spicy so the red-cooked pork, he doesn't get because it's slightly sweet."

"Needs more spicy!" interjected Fat Man Scoop, a.k.a. Rabbi.

"No, I disagree. This red-cooked pork is just as special as the bitter melon because it, too, is entirely new. You have combined certain techniques from your experience with Taiwanese *lu wei* and also Hunan style red-cooked pork, but this is undoubtedly your dish. It could only come from your experience."

Startled at the compliment he just paid me, I deflected and made the conversation about Fish.

"Fish, I'm curious. What do you do? Like for a job. Are you a food writer?"

"No. I drive the general and give tours of Tibet."

"This is a very specific experience as well."

For a kid who spent most of his life in an Orlando cul-de-sac, it was a revelation to be back on the mothership—to come home and touch the culture I knew was part of me but never fully understood and maybe still don't. It was a testament to the universality of culture and identity and values that a Chinese seed could be blown out to a cul-de-sac in Orlando, Florida, via Taiwan, and still grow to be understood by its brethren back on the mothership. The force is strong and the Empire will never erase us.

I became confident that if I had kids with Dena that were half-Chinese/Taiwanese, half-Irish/Italian, I'd still be reflected in them. But

---

* Chowhound.

then I started thinking if it was egotistical to desire reflection in another human being. What if I just let it go? What if I just trusted that if I set my essence free into another human being that it would be taken to places and people and dishes that I couldn't imagine? I once again remembered DMX* and thought to myself: how far does the bitter melon go?

_____

* "If you love something let it go, if it comes back to you, it's yours. If it doesn't, it never was." —DMX, who also makes an appearance in *Fresh Off the Boat* for the same quote.

PART 2

LAST DAYS ALONE

Corky

The nice way to describe Shanghai would be "Westernized," but if you sit a first-generation Shanghainese-American parent down and ask them about their children or Shanghai after watching a subpar episode of *The Voice China*, they'll probably mutter something closer to "compromised."

I went to Shanghai because it was supposed to be the city in China that most paralleled my existence. Not just because of its red-cooked pork, but also because of its compromises. I dreaded going, but standing on the wave of my latest revelations, I didn't want to fall back into the trap of villainizing the West. Being Western wasn't Shanghai's problem, conforming to a larger global normalizing of identity was. Shanghai felt like a constant, depressing reminder of what we were all becoming: an international class of third culture kids. But before the third culture extinguished old Shanghai, I was determined to find it one last time using the same thing that allowed me to tell my story in America: red-cooked pork.

I have to admit that even Old Shanghai was compromised in its way. I'm no historian, but I find it impossible to talk about Shanghai's modern development without first noting that it took place largely under the spell of opium. I spent one summer of my life smoking black tar opium, and I can tell you that anything is possible with the Big O, except voluntary action. You can lie in your bed drooling on a pillow dreaming up plans for the new Death Star, but actually picking up a pen and drafting those plans is humanly impossible. You may think that the force is strong and that you are lifting all the furniture in your room off the ground, but I promise you NOTHING is moving in that room, especially not your bowels, because you probably won't shit for a week while smoking opium. (This is why I believe the opening lyrics to House of Pain's "Jump Around" are about opium constipation.)* I say all this to make the point that while Great Britain may not have actually and intentionally opiate-raped us, intentions really don't matter when your actions in fact render someone helpless and involuntary.

And to what do we owe this incredible opium slumber? *A trade deficit resulting from the exchange of tea.* British people fucked with tea so heavy that even though they were on the gold standard, they'd go switch their money up for silver from other countries to exchange with China for tea. There was a huge deficit because there wasn't shit that Chinese people or the rest of the world for that matter wanted from England. If China were trading with France, this never would have happened, because France has shit you might actually want. Oh, croissants, Viognier from the northern Rhone, and gelatinous foods like head cheese? Yes, I'll trade you some high mountain oolong tea. England was probably rollin' up on countries like, "Excuse me, kind sir, could I interest you in jellied eels, medieval torture weapons, or English springer spaniels?" SON, we got GREMLINS, shih tzus, and you know EWOKS are from China, right? The fuck do we need spaniels for?

Regardless, China got fucked up heavy because England started growing opium in India and dumping it on Shanghai in exchange for tea. When the Qing dynasty tried to stop the trade of opium, England pretended not to understand why anyone would want to stop the whole-sale unloading of narcotics on their population. This would literally be Tijuana throwing its arms up at the U.S. like, "What? We can't just send heroin to L.A. for pastrami from Langer's? This is entirely unreasonable."

After numerous wars, settlements, and treaties, Shanghai became the most "open" city in China. Economically at least, it's no longer consti-pated. It is probably the most diverse in terms of non-Chinese residents and tourists, although some areas of China are more varied in their mix

---

* Pack it up, pack it in, let me begin. . . .

of Chinese ethnic groups. In Shanghai you have the Bund,* you have Laowai Jie (literally, "Foreigner Street"), and restaurants and sucky-sucky spots that cater to foreign businessmen. While separate and unequal race-based segregation is commonplace in America—ethnic food aisles, Inglewood, and Queensbridge,† where we set aside our shittiest spaces for black people and immigrants to enjoy foods that increase the probability of heart disease—China puts its best foot forward when carving up its cities for foreign vultures. One by-product of all this is third culture kids.

Corky Shu is a third culture kid. I met him sometime in early 2013 on Doyers Street in Manhattan outside Excellent Pork Chop House. He was carrying bags of sneakers and skateboards he'd just gotten from Supreme. If you drew a stencil outlining Corky in that moment, he could have been the Hypebeast Jumpman logo. Truth be told, I could be the logo two days out of the week as well, but like a dog that could smell another dog with the same disease, I knew what Corky had and steered clear.

A few months later, I was sitting in Chengdu Instagramming the red-cooked pork I'd made at Hakka Homes, asking if anyone in China wanted to "TEST THE CHAMPION SOUND." Random commenters left messages telling me to try Old Jesse, Fu 1088, and a few other Shanghainese spots with red-cooked pork. Of course, red-cooked pork originates from Shanghai, and as a practitioner of Hunan-style red-cooked pork, I wanted to try the best.

I was also impressed by how many people out there on Instagram were ready to help me find Shanghai's best red-cooked pork. So, I enlisted the internets to help me once again, this time with a more serious problem: watching internet porn.

The first response I got was a message from Corky.

---

* Historical banking district on the water in central Shanghai.

† Sarcasm . . . the difference between the neighborhoods carved out for white people in China and black people in America is that China shows off for white people, while the nicest thing America's dropped off in the hood are Clark Wallabees, which Ghostface has to paint blue and cream to be any type of wearable.

What's good? You outchea? Hit me, homie. I'm in Shanghai.

Yea I don't know anyone out there, so lemme know.

Ha ha. Come to the Hai this weekend. You should've been here last weekend, was kind of crazy.

Ignoring his attempt at afflicting me with FOMO,* I disregarded his comment and got to the important things in life.

Yo, what are the Bangbros-type sites in China? All my shit is blocked.

LOL. You need a VPN to get on Twitter, Facebook, etc. Try and download Astrill and see if you can buy a month subscription.

What's a VPN? All I need is Bangbros and World Star.

A VPN gives you a different IP address so all those websites aren't blocked. It tells the China firewall that you're logged on from the U.S.

Aight, I'ma hit you when I'm in Shanghai. Also, I wanna try the best *hong sau rou*. Shanghai style. Any ideas? I was thinking old *xin ji*.

Bet. Come through. I got no hooks there, but I can call and make a reservation for you and talk to them ahead of time. Hit me on WhatsApp if you need anything.

---

*   Fear of missing out.

I landed in Shanghai a few days later, dropped my bags at my hotel, then went to meet Corky with Evan in tow. He had told us to meet him in the lobby of this hotel called the Puli, which I immediately liked 'cause it rhymed with *coolie* and *coochie* and "Oochie Wally," but I don't think they've ever played "Oochie Wally" at this joint. The lobby was cold, sterile, and uninviting: typical modern Shanghai. A grand hotel lobby outfitted with dark minimalism and square leather club chairs that dared you to sit in them.

So many of Shanghai's high-end experiences seem derived from the Forbidden City: ninety-nine ways to make you feel like a eunuch in the presence of the divine. I was crunchy as I cut through the Puli lobby, and then I saw Corky. He had shaggy hair with a white tee, basketball shorts, and Margicla Chuck Taylors.

Corky had a strange crew in tow. An ad agency couple from New York, a henchman from work, and some other "influencers" in town for some sort of activewear conference in Shanghai. Having not spoken English to anyone besides Evan in a week, it was weird to be suddenly facing New York in Shanghai.

"This is Cramer and his wife. They're—"

Cramer lunged forward.

"Yo! You know my boy, from—"

He was interrupted by his friend.

"Dude, Vice is blowing up, man! Congrats on . . ."

I tuned out. I knew exactly what was happening, and I was regretting it already. I just did the immigrant smile, shook hands, and avoided any sort of real conversation. I thought about bailing on dinner and just exploring Shanghai on my own. While the others studied the art on the walls, I leaned over to Evan.

"Yo, Ev, we should just get outta here, man. This is one of those fuccboi business dinners."

"Yeah, this is googin-faced, but I think it'd be pretty rude if you just left, man."

The plan was to eat at Madam Zhu's, an upmarket restaurant in a mall you reached via escalator. Zhu's was very cinematic: it sought to suspend your disbelief and transport you to an amalgamation of outdoor Chengdu teahouses and a Shanghainese salon, but the restaurant was such a big, bright, white box that it just felt empty and contrived. At Zhu's nothing was suspended, my disbelief was constant, and I remained persistently aware I was eating in a fucking mall.

There were classic dishes on Madam Zhu's menu, like roast duck and lion's head meatballs, with some updated joints thrown in like wok-tossed cauliflower, snow-pea-shoot fried rice, and a decent rendition of red-cooked pork. I liked that they served nouveau iterations of dishes you'd make out of necessity at home, such as the pea-shoot fried rice, alongside classic banquet dishes.

Growing up, you never saw pea-shoot fried rice on a restaurant menu. It had no protein! There weren't even eggs! What up with the scallions doe, doggy? No, pea-shoot fried rice looked like green Filipino garlic fried rice: broke, one ingredient, struggle carbs. But like Filipino garlic fried rice, it came out of an experience. We had pea-shoot fried rice when Moms forgot to buy eggs or we ran out of eggs or when the only thing in the fridge was pea shoots and old rice. So you make it happen, and after it happens consistently over the course of your entire childhood, you start to crave pea-shoot fried rice. Through the last half decade in China and Taiwan, I saw pea-shoot fried rice pop up sporadically in fine restaurants, and it's proven every single time to be the perfect carb. Pea-shoot fried rice was officially good enough to put on the table in the presence of guests who hadn't been over to the crib since the Opium Wars. Whether Madam Zhu's was reflecting an experience or reflecting other menus, I didn't care. I was proud to see home cooking on the menu. Ninja, we made it.

"What you think about the food, fam?" asked Corky.

"It's on point. Evan, make sure to get photos of the *mi tze huo twai*, they bury it in sugar on sticky rice. Haven't seen that in a while. Also, the flounder is Shanghai-style but a lot more *tsao lu* and soy sauce than usual. Definitely makes it a richer dish. Same with their sea cucumber, I think they thicken it with roe and the brown sauce is a gravy. Shanghai-nese food here is a bit more cloying, but deep."

"Got it."

Corky watched us taking notes.

"Damn, y'all do this everywhere?"

"Yup." Evan somehow conveyed negative excitement.

"Actually, scratch that, Evan. It's shrimp roe, not fish roe. Fish roe would be bigger."

"Yes, boss."

I could tell Evan was annoyed and embarrassed to be taking notes at dinner. It was constantly a point of contention. Corky laughed. "Evan the henchman over here."

I didn't laugh.

"Nah, we're partners."

As the dishes kept coming, I noticed that the chef had a steady hand, precise execution, balanced flavors, and a flair for creativity when the situation called for it, but not gratuitously. The level of skill was incredibly high. Madam Zhu's actually had the same goals as modern "Asian" restaurants in America, i.e., to bring the culture of dark people to upwardly mobile people, but they didn't clumsily push Chinese food through a French ricer. While the dining room suffered from Sichuanese theatrics and big-box Western comforts, the plate was unscathed. Most dishes used the tried and true techniques, keeping their identities intact for third culture consumption. Some even refined those techniques. I found it entirely more enjoyable to eat scallion oil chicken at Madam Zhu's with the scallions and ginger cut 80 percent thinner than they are at Noodletown in N.Y. or any Hong Kong–style cafe. It's just sad that we didn't do it until we had guests over.*

I enjoyed Madam Zhu's even though it was part of the Kitchen Consensus: You can't escape the square plate, the reduction, the removal of bones, or the white patrons who consume culture along lines demar-

---

* Foreigners.

cated by a tire manufacturer. At times, I find myself reading this tire manufacturer's guidelines on how, when, where, what, and why to dine and almost always disagree. From Martin Luther's Ninety-Five Theses to the Confucian Analects to the Michelin Guide, they're all just listicles mobilizing the middle* in an effort to create a consensus. I'd say I hate the consensus, but it's impossible to hate something that doesn't exist. Whether it's Washington, D.C., Middle East peace, or a true shooting percentage, there is no such thing as a consensus, just the idea of one. But chasing the consensus has derailed us since the beginning.

I don't like tablecloths, I don't subscribe to the idea that there's one objective way to be excellent, I don't like when an international class of moneyed people dictates the way we present local cultures, but I liked Madam Zhu's. I liked it because it didn't sacrifice the identity of the food. There wasn't that feeling you get in some "starred" restaurants that the world has passed you by, that properly steaming scallion chicken is a lost art, that shortcuts were taken in service of the bottom line but disservice of the craft. At Madam Zhu's, the pasteurization didn't usurp the thing being pasteurized.

Madam Zhu's put Chinese food in a handsome suit with wide lapels, three buttons, and a vest, but the dressing room never fully took over the dining room. The food wasn't some sort of goofy kung fu–inspired formal wear or an imperial tuxedo with wizard sleeves and silk lining. Madam Zhu's recognized that, yes, I am a Chinese restaurant; yes, there are times in life where you have to do business over scallion oil chicken with a suit; but, no, I don't need a suit that makes me look like Jet Li at Sundance. I am a Chinaman. I have a suit. Please enjoy the view.

---

* This is one reason why I'm glad I live in this era versus any other. I exist at a point in history where you can actually be ignorant of the middle, create for the margins, and live in a rabbit hole because of the internet. There are so many tentacles that grow from each and every subculture that if you want, you can make a living on any point of your countercultural spiderweb of choice. That is, until your industry actually makes an impact, crosses over, and attracts new followers, who unfortunately don't want to understand the culture from its genesis and follow the throughline, but instead step into the arena and present their Ninety-Five Theses for how your culture should now be consumed.

———

Right when I was starting to settle into Shanghai and a delightful food coma, Cramer brought me back to Earth.

"*FU REN! FU REN!*"* screamed Cramer.

As his voice rang through the restaurant, waiters, bussers, food runners, and managers spun around. There was chaos. Sound the alarm! There are unsatisfied white people 'round these parts! Simultaneously, three servicemen and -women made their moves toward Cramer. It was a race to the third waypoint, where it would become clear who was in the best position to reach Cramer first. The other two saw that the third, a nice woman with her hair in a bun, would be closest in proximity to satisfying Cramer.

"Man, I love China! It's the fucking best. You yell 'FU REN' and they all come running like roaches!"

Evan already knew. He gave me a poke, a look, and every nonverbal communication known to man, pleading with me to not jump over the table and strangle Cramer like I was Far East Coast Latrell Sprewell.

Think about it. A country welcomes you with open arms. An entire civilization of people look at themselves shamefully, motivate themselves to do better, to make themselves presentable, train their people to be at your beck and call, do their best to gain your respect, but instead of being filled with humbling gratitude that all of this is for you, you toy with them. You yell "*FU REN!*" like it's some sort of game, just to see how fast people will run toward you in an effort to serve. Why? For your ego? For a quick laugh? To remind everyone who the fuck you are? We'll never understand white people, but still we try.

"Hi, meester, yes, I'm sorry, what can I helps you with?" said the waitress.

"Oh, nothing, I just, you know, ha ha. I'm fucking with you. Everything is great. The food is great. We're having a great time! The service is incredible."

———

* In Mandarin, it means "service person" or "waiter."

"OK, good! I am glad you are enjoy it. Let me know if you need anything."

I was on the verge of losing my shit. I wanted to go all Dad and flip the dinner table because I suddenly felt like everything about Shanghai was fucked. From the opium wars to the stupid duty-free hotel lobby to fucking Cramer. I suddenly felt the urge to exterminate the entire city of these ungrateful foreign roaches. But Corky knew better. He gave me a look, motioned with his hands to calm down, and whispered to me, "Chill, fam. . . . I know." I didn't know this guy at all, but something about him said he knew. In times of hate and pain, that'll hold a madman over.

"Cramer, you wildin', man," I said.

"What do you mean? It's awesome, dude. China's the best! People bust their ass for anything."

"You fuckin' with them, though!"

"Yeah, a little bit, but it's their job! I'm just having fun with 'em."

I stared at him for a second and chose to let it go. I knew. Corky knew. Cramer? Left behind. It was the most Chinese thing I've ever done: just keep walking.* Five thousand years of history isn't going to stop for Cramer.

Corky picked up the check, Cramer ended up buying me a Häagen Dazs banana split downstairs, and everyone said their goodbyes, but Corky hung around after everyone else left to walk Evan and me to the hotel. We sat on a bench outside the mall for a minute, watching Shanghai go by.

"You good, man?"†

"Fuck Cramer."

Corky laughed, then put his hand on my shoulder.

---

* Johnnie Walker with *wang lao ji* at karaoke is also the most Chinese drink.

† I've known Corky for about a year now and it's always dope when he hits me, 'cause the first thing he asks is, "You good, man?" Not in a "What's up?" way or just casual checking-in way, he genuinely wants to know how people are doing, and it's rare. I respect it. I respect it a lot.

"Yo, it's light, man. Cramer's just Cramer. He don't mean anything. Dude has no idea."

"It ain't right, though."

"Naw, it definitely ain't right, but what are you gonna do? Get ugly to teach him a lesson? Then you in the wrong."

"He bought you an ice cream," Evan chimed in.

"It's so Chinese how we handled that. The answer to everything is to let people spit on you."

Evan rose up from the bench outside the mall and declared: "China's doing its thing now, man. People can laugh at China, but we know what time it is."

I agreed with Evan. China had been putting its head down, biting its tongue, and waiting its turn for the last hundred years. Anyone who still wanted to laugh at us like we're still stuck on the opiates had a rapidly approaching expiration date.

"You're all right, man," I said to Corky.

"Me?" asked Corky.

"Yeah, you all right."

"Oh, thank you, *da gu*," he said sarcastically.

"Naw, not like that. I didn't know you, man. I just met you, but you aight, man. Thanks for keepin' me from flipping the dinner table."

"Got you, fam."

"Where you from?" I asked.

"D.C., just like you, homie."

"Word? D.C. your whole life?"

"D.C., then Beijing for middle school, then back in D.C., then went to Florida like you. Been in Shanghai last few years workin'."

"Damn, son, you for real one of them third culture kids."

"I guess so."

"Proper Shanghainese, ha ha."

"Naw, Hunan Ren."

"Stop playin'! Hunan?"

"Yup, Pops is Hunan Ren, so I'm Hunan Ren, just like you."

"Damn, what up, twin!"

"Let's get up tomorrow. Get some rest. I'll pick you up at the hotel, show you around the city."

"No doubt. Thanks, fam."

The next morning Corky pulled up to my hotel in a S500 with a driver bumpin' Migos.

"We doin' it like this?"

"*Lao ban* steez.* You guys hungry?"

"Yeah, man, I stay missin' the continental breakfast in the morning."

"Where's Evan?"

"Oh shit, I think he's working on Baohaus 2011 taxes upstairs. I'll call him."

Baohaus 2011 taxes were a sore spot between Evan and me. It was a problem we both contributed to. For the first two years we owned Baohaus, we didn't have money for a bookkeeper, so we just put all the receipts and invoices in a box vowing to organize them at some point between tomorrow and the end of civilization as we know it. Of course, we didn't get to it in time for tax season and had to file for an extension. When we finally did file with the homies at Jackson Hewitt, we got audited because we were a cash business that didn't have the proper documentation for a lot of transactions. I stuck Evan with getting the paperwork together because I was still cooking at the restaurant while also writing *Fresh Off the Boat*. Neither of us wanted to deal with it, but since I was the boss, I just told him he had to and of course, he resented it.

I called him from Corky's car.

"Evan, you wanna come eat?"

"Yeah, but I'm working on the taxes."

"Ehhh, just work on it later, let's go hang with Corky."

"Dude, you're gonna be up my ass if I don't finish this."

"Yeah, you gotta finish before we leave China, but what's one day? We're only in Shanghai for a week, you can do it in Chengdu."

---

*   Big boss style.

"OK, gimme five minutes."

The first place Corky took us to was Yang's, an institution for *sin jian bao* (pan-fried dumplings), which are to the dumpling canon what Chicago-style deep dish is to pizza. Depending on where you get them, the dough may be thick and closer to the sugar dough used for *char siu bao* or *mantou* than it is to a dumpling skin. But *sin jian bao* done right gives you the best of both worlds, with a bun on top cooked through by the steam and a greasy thick bottom with the crunch of a Giordano's crust. Some places create a thinner, southern Chinese–style dumpling skin resembling a crispy Lou Malnati's butter crust, but my preference is a thicker, northern-style dumpling skin, cooked al dente with just enough chew and a firm bottom with a dark sear that resembles the great Dominic Di Fara's Sicilian slice.

Yang's had a thinner skin, not much bounciness, but a great sear on the bottom and a generous portion of pork filling resembling a lion's head meatball bursting with juices. The amount of ginger, rice wine, and scallions was perfect in the filling, and after a couple, I was sprung. In that particular style with a thin skin, Yang's was tops. I think Yang's also sets the Guinness world record for proportion of MSG to surface area for a single item of food. After three dumplings, my mouth was dumb dry, and my head was spinning like I had just eaten a spoonful of cinnamon mixed with coffee grounds.

"Damn, son, this shit is O.D. with the MSG."

"You gonna shit your pants, too."

"They got laxatives in this pork?"

"I don't know, but you definitely gonna shit your pants."

"Is it the oil?" Evan guessed.

"No idea, man. It might just be that there's so much food in one dumpling, maybe it's the grease, maybe it got laxatives, nobody knows, but you will catch a Yang's shit right quick."

"This is dope, but I could only eat this a few times a year."

"No doubt. I don't even really eat Chinese food," said Corky.

"How you don't eat Chinese food and you in Shanghai?" I asked.

"I just feel gross after, man. Some restaurants use recycled oil and even if it's not recycled, it's still greasy. There's always MSG. The quality of meat is sus. I'm over it. You gotta eat at chains out here."

"I don't know, dude. In Chengdu, we eat on the street. In Shanghai a few years ago, I ate all around the streets. It's that bad?"

"You live here long enough, you learn not to fuck with street food. You'll catch one real quick."

"That just seems crazy, though, to live in China and not eat Chinese food."

"How long you here?"

"Eight weeks."

"You'll see. You holler at me in eight weeks."

I took a sip of my diet Coke, let it settle, and as I stopped to think about it, something came over me. After a pause, I gave in.

"I'ma have to holler at you in eight minutes 'cause I gotta find a bathroom right now."

"TOLD YOU!"

After a wild public-restroom interlude, we ate again.

Corky didn't want to eat out of stalls, so he took us to Tim's, a Cantonese spot from Hong Kong that was Michelin-rated, but just like Madam Zhu's, I was impressed. Michelin stars or not, the food was at least three emoji flames. Perfect *char siu* pork just firm enough to keep all the juices intact, dripping with candied lard over a crispy dark brown crust dotted with bits of char. The roast suckling pig was just the same. Perfect slices of pork—firm and supple but forgiving at first bite. The pork projected a veneer of excellence that I found intimidating, yet bite after bite was softer than the last. It was absolutely perfect Cantonese roast pork, but truth be told, the perfection pissed me off.

These motherfuckers had a crystal prawn dish where the prawn was cleaned to the point where there was no hint of red. It was pure white snow in the form of a prawn. It had a snappy, bouncy, satisfying exterior, which made it taste more like lobster than any lobster I'd ever eaten in my life. Using just his skill, this fool was able to turn shrimp into fucking lobster. I thought alchemy in China was relegated to making fake eggs or lions,* but, clearly, when the skills were applied in a positive manner the result was transcendent. I was still tight, though.

"This food was made by cyborgs."

"Or Japanese people," said Evan.

"Ha, why you mad, though?" asked Corky.

"It's so consistent. Every bite is the same perfect piece of pork or shrimp-lobster. It's upsetting. I want to know how this motherfucker did this."

"You the chef, man. Figure it out."

"I mean, I'm gonna go home and try, but I'm going to fail a lot before I figure it out."

"Well, if you *can* figure it out, then why you so impressed?"

"Because I wouldn't even have the idea to do this until I saw it. The level of detail on the idea for this shrimp is insane. Your boy 'Tim' woke up and was like: I will make Sonic the Hedgehog shrimp that tastes like lobster. This is ALCHEMY. I can't make tea into coffee or coffee into Kahlua, but this fool can make prawns into lobster. It's insane."

Once again, I had to accept that Chinamen looked good in suits and that food really popped against the white backdrop of a tablecloth. And once again it bothered me. Did my constant fear of assimilation and foreign interference come from being a child of the rootless diaspora? I wasn't sure, but I did what I always did when I found myself falling for an upwardly mobile lifestyle: I ran downstairs.

"Corky, I fux with this. But I need to eat local, b. What up with the local Shanghainese food, homie?"

"Well, we gonna do Fu 1088," Corky responded.

Fu 1088? At this point, I had to rally the troops. I decided to deliver the monologue of a lifetime, or at least of this visit to Shanghai. I channeled the British Tory in me that resists appropriation, cooptation, gentrification, boutique barbers, artisanal chili oil, ring spun cotton, the dreaded "elevation" of cultural wares, and progress of all types. Whatever

---

* There was a zoo in China that had a Tibetan mastiff posing as a lion in an exhibit.

happened to wearing a good ol' made-in-China pre-shrunk tee asking "What's poppin', slime?" with hair clippings and chili oil stains? I went in.

"Sure, we gonna do Fu 1088, but that joint got a minimum per head, wild Adobe Flash pop-up windows on the website, and it'll be with your Converse homies. We need to eat somewhere with fucking landlines, twenty-four K dial up, physical newspapers, and ninjas with Earthlink emails. I'm tryna see Xanga pages, *The Sporting News*, red-cooked pork, *kau fu*, stir-fried yellow eels with chives, and other archaic homestyle delights. I wanna see Gremlin keepers behind the register. WE USED TO BE THE STREETS, DOG. WHERE WE AT NOW? WHERE THE LAZY SUSANS? CAN A BROTHER EAT OFF A LAZY SUSAN? THE CHOPSTICKS AIN'T BAMBOO HERE! I NEED SPLINTERS IN MY FINGERS."

"Aight. Aight! You're crazy, man. But I got you *xiong di*. . . ."

We agreed to go to Old Jesse (Lao Ji Shi), which the internet and Corky both told me was the place to go for a proper Shanghainese home-style meal. There was talk of yellow eels, crab-meat sauce silken tofu, burnt-scallion codfish heads, and, of course, the most famous Shanghai-nese red-cooked pork in the world. In the meantime, Corky showed me around Shanghai the rest of the day.

We found ourselves at a bootleg DVD store where I bought out their entire collection of John Cusack and Ryan Gosling movies for about $10 total. We brought our DVDs across to the foot massage joint, and had the ill lemon tea, milk toast, *guiling gao** foot massage man-date, watching the terrible *Only God Forgives*. Over the course of a week, I had unwit-tingly become fast friends with Corky and didn't think twice about hav-ing deep personal conversations while someone living at the Chinese poverty line sanded the calluses off my heel. Eventually, I ran out of things to talk about and showed him a picture of Dena.

"She's not my type, but she's cute," he said.

"Yeah?"

"Yeah, I like girls that are mixed race."

---

* Tortoise jelly.

"She's Italian-Irish."

"I like half-Asian and something else. My last girl was Asian and French."

"Hmmm, lemme take a look at her."

Corky pulled up a photo of his ex on Instagram.

"Yo, that chick follows me on Instagram, b."

"For real?"

"Yeah, man, she fly."

"She follows you, though?"

"Yeah, son, she be leaving comments, too."

Corky was disturbed.

Once Corky told me he preferred mixed-race Asian women, I paused. Usually if a friend told me they preferred dating someone of the same race or background, they spoke about family values and shared history. It usually wasn't a conversation about the physical similarities as much as it was comfort and acceptance or at least assumed understanding. That wasn't what Corky was talking about. For him, it was a look; Corky wanted banh mi or maybe just a third culture kind of love.

It made me think about why I liked Dena. I guess white girls with pink nipples and tiger stripes were a type that I liked subconsciously? OK, truth be told, it was a type I specifically searched for on xvideos.com, but in real life I kept it wide open. Even in digital life on OKCupid, I started clicking every ethnicity except white when setting my preferences because I *knew* that whiteness had an unfair advantage in my mind. Since I can remember, I'd been told that white women were superior, even from my Asian parents. If it wasn't Chinese, please be white. It was a feeling I'd tried to filter out since sixth grade.

In sixth grade, there was a girl named Brooke Something that every-one agreed was the "logo": blond, tall, skinny, and could undoubtedly call out a pea under a waterbed. Brooke wore her uniform polo buttoned up and proper with long lanky arms slinking out like no. 10 spaghetti. There was always a crowd of people around, and she stood a head taller, gliding across the playground like she was Princess Diana. I never saw her frazzled, never saw her off-center, but then again I never really saw her. She was camera-ready in the sixth grade, giving everyone a glance, a smile, but never really connecting. Brooke kind of just gave the Miss America wave, avoiding any real eye contact. She was everything Nickelodeon told us we were supposed to like, and we did.

But then something happened. A few months into the school year, I was waiting to use the bathroom before class, hopping around on one leg trying to hold it in, when the door opened. Without thinking, I just bumrushed the door and stumbled onto the baddest chick I'd ever seen. I backed up, still squeezing my crotch to keep the ammonia in place, when we locked eyes. Cot damn. There she was, shiny black hair, piercing dark brown eyes, polo shirt tucked in sideways, with her skirt hiked up, lookin' at me cockeyed. Her name was Lourdes Perez.

She adjusted herself, patted down her skirt, tossed her hair, and made way for me into the latrine. I didn't move. Paralyzed, my urge to piss faded as I caught the *illest* boner of my young life. For a moment, I understood sex. It wasn't about false ideals and pedestals or cupped-hand waving; it was primal, instinctual, and visceral. It grabs you at the bottom of your balls, and it's undeniable. When it's right, there's no type. And now I know why the coquí frog* sings. . . .

You talk about values or shared histories or similar life goals after the fact. They're things you talk about when someone asks why you got chose, and I guess they're things that sustain a relationship after the choosing, as if it was a business. Come to think of it, marriage is a business. It may be a partnership if it's equal, or an S Corp if one person is more dominant, or even an LLC if liability is the primary concern, but love? Love is a different thing. For me, it starts with lust, and I don't see anything wrong with it. They say it's "so hard not to act reckless,"† but here's the problem. It's all reckless.

When the pedicure was over, I was pressed for success.

---

*   Coquí frogs are native to Puerto Rico and get dumb loud hollering at shawties.

†   Kanye.

"I'm glad my heels are gonna be extra presentable in Jumpman slides at Old Jesse tonight," I crowed.

"Why you gotta be so ratchet, fam? You have two hundred pairs of sneakers and you wear these dirty-ass slides everywhere. Aren't those your shower sandals?"

"They comfortable. I'm 'bout that cozy boy life, so I stay in these sandals. And why can't you just let my heels shine? My heels haven't been this shiny since I had my feet up on my mother's placenta."

"I mean, if you wanna go eat dinner at a Shanghainese institution in shower sandals, that's your prerogative."

"Motherfucker, did you just Bobby Brown me?"

"I ain't Bobby Brown you. I'm just questioning your choice of footwear."

"You said this spot is the hood champ with old Chinamen prepping food, killing eels, and peeling snow peas on crates in the alley."

"We eating with Janice and Eddie. Their parents own Golden Eagle, man."

"Is that some super buffet?"

"No, dick, it's the biggest holding company of malls in the world, I think."

"Wait, we're eating with the Chinese Eddie DeBartolos?"

"Pretty much."

"Cot damn, Corky, you just ruined this date! I thought we were gonna pick our toenails, smell our fingers, roll up our wife-beaters, and eat homestyle Shanghainese food. Eating with mall magnates is not romantic to me."

"This is Shanghai, man. It's not like that. And I'm not like that."

Later that night, Corky, Evan, and I rolled up on Old Jesse, and in many ways it felt just like pulling up to Rao's on 114th Street in East Harlem. A small group of people were loitering outside waiting for tables, but it was a different type of line than the peons waiting for cheeseburgers and crinkle-cut fries in Madison Square Park. If you didn't know somebody, you weren't going to know the world's greatest red-cooked pork. The group of people, all friends of the restaurant, consisted mainly of well-heeled guests with Gucci loafers and children in Flyknit Chukkas, all wearing strange combinations of Joyrich and Rick Owens.

It was a second-generation Shanghainese scene with "We Made It"* parents who probably remember peeling snow peas and slicing eels but now brought their private-school children who prefer McRibs and KFC Egg Tarts to pay respects to the culture. Instead of incense in their hands, they held PSPs and bowed dismissively like Larry David.†

"China is a country full of only children serviced by six adults," said Corky.

"What are you talking about?"

"The one-child policy, dude. You can only have one kid, so that one kid over there has two parents and four grandparents that put all their money, energy, and hopes on him. Everyone is a golden child in this country."

"Damn, it's a whole country of Evans!"

"Shut up, man!" screamed the Golden Child.

"It's all good, I'm a golden child, too," Corky said.

We walked in, past the curtain in the doorway and landed on Mars. From the amber lighting to the smell of Shanghainese cooking wine playing with Chinkiang vinegar and the *Scent of a Woman* poster in the bathroom, Old Jesse is a moment that you see in black-and-white photos, hear about from aunts and uncles that got away, and talk about like some kind of Far East Coast prerevolutionary Cuba. A romantic twenty-seat restaurant Chinese people fled to for one last rendezvous with their boos before getting sentenced to life in an arranged marriage.

As soon as I walked in, I knew I was in for one of those meals where the chef has it all on a string. Like Isiah Thomas dancing through the lane without losing his handle or Ronaldinho cruising across the pitch

---

* More Jadakiss.

† One of my favorite episodes of *Curb* is when Larry gets called out for giving a dismissive bow.

with that Brazilian foot wizardry, Old Jesse had it on a fucking string. From the fried eels lacquered in sweet braising sauce to the *kau fu* to the crabmeat on tofu, everything was as you imagined it jumping out of old Fu Pei Mei cookbooks. These were all dishes I'd had in their home-cooked variation. Every aunt or uncle could produce *one* of these dishes at a high level and bring it to potluck, but to have it all laid out at the same time, at the right temperature, at the highest level, was unprecedented for me. It was like watching LeBron take over Game 6 against the Spurs in 2013 like I always knew he could, rise to the expectations, and crush anything we ever thought was possible in basketball. Old Jesse presented Chinese food in a way I'd never experienced but always imagined.

The signature dish was the codfish head that you had to order ahead of time. No one in the restaurant would reveal how it was prepared, but I suspected it was a steamed head finished with hot oil, topped with burned scallions and a nod to the gods. It was superb.

"How does it compare to the Chinese food you've had in your travels?" Janice asked.

"I mean. This is ground zero. There are certain dishes I've had better in a handful of places, like the lion's head meatballs, and I've had good *kau fu*. I have been able to make yellow eels with chives as good as this probably once in my life because all the stars aligned and we had *tsao lu* in Orlando, but it was after a lot of mistakes. To see every dish here done at the highest level I've probably ever seen it all on one table is pretty fucking insane."

"Well, I know you're known for red-cooked pork, so I'm curious what you think about that."

Fuck. I almost forgot. I felt like a pig being fed for slaughter. Caught up in Old Jesse's rapture, I forgot what I had come for.

I forgot because over the course of the week, I'd eaten red-cooked pork at every restaurant that had it on the menu. Fu 1088, a restaurant with a per person minimum and extra crispy white tablecloth, had one of the most texturally impressive red-cooked pork dishes I've ever had, but fell short with a sauce that broke down, yielding a layer of oil on top and a flavor that left me wanting more acid. Other, more homestyle places had soulful braising liquids but left a lot to be desired texturally. Nothing blew us away or made us reconsider our methods. Neither Evan nor I was ready to give up the garlic and dry red chili that made Hunan-style red-cooked pork famous or the cherry cola that defined our Taiwanese-Hunan-American version that we served in a bao at our shop. And then it appeared.

You couldn't have scripted it any better. Shining, dark, red lacquered pork belly in a clay pot. No garnish, no modernized presentation, no insecurity about doing it the same way for decades, just picture perfect Shanghainese *hong sau rou*: the holy grail of holiday food.

"Motherfuckers," I said.

"Damn, son, I need a photo of this," said Evan.

"Dig in," said Janice with a smile.

This was it. This is what happens if there is a heaven. You show up in shower sandals, god gives you back the wallet you lost in El Segundo, and then she offers you a piece of the mystical red-cooked pork you've heard about all your life.

I took a bite, and my teeth melted through three inches of pork belly like a broadsword in butter. The sugar came first, tempered by superior dark soy sauce, buttressed by the undeniable flavor of freshly slaughtered pork from a three-year-old pig, with rice wine dancing all over it like a Lavo waitress with sparklers in her hands. Just when you thought it was over, like you'd totally lost your mind and fallen miles down a pork belly hole, there was Bird once again. The Chinkiang vinegar was like listening to Charlie Parker with strings—it caught me and reinforced that no, I hadn't died and fallen down a one-note pork belly hole with sparkler wielding bimbos but was in fact still in the motherfucking building and that this *hong sau rou* is real. I understood Shanghainese *hong sau rou*. It didn't need garlic and chilis because the song was about sugar, rice wine, superior dark soy, pork essence, and the way they all played with Chinkiang black vinegar. Every ensemble has its configuration, and so does red-cooked pork.

"Damn, son. Lost one."

For a moment, Janice was pleased. She'd taken me to a place that schooled me on my signature dish. But just as I was going to concede the 2000 election, Evan came bursting through headquarters with the latest numbers.

"It's cloying. You can't eat more than one piece of it," said Evan as he licked the veneer of his teeth.

"Well, *hong sau rou* is an indulgent dish, one piece is probably enough!" countered Janice.

"Nah, people come to Baohaus, and they'll eat three to five baos EASY. If we used pork like this, no one would eat more than one."

I took another bite . . . then another bite . . . and then still another bite. Each one with diminishing returns.

"You know, I feel like the vinegar is the thing that keeps you coming back. The sugar is too much, the pork fat is great, the texture is phenomenal, but you start to come back less and less."

"Yeah, for sure the vinegar is the thing that they do, which I think really sets it off, but Hunan *hong sau rou* has the garlic, the chilis, and you even hit it with some peppercorns that give it an air of menthol. Shanghainese *hong sau rou* leaves the sugar out to dry with just vinegar and wine. It's cloying," said Evan.

He may have been right. But even if the red-cooked pork was one note with a countermove, it worked. Like Shaq's drop-step spin to a baby hook, Old Jesse's pork had only one countermove: vinegar. Our Hunan red-cooked pork was like the Nigerian Nightmare, Hakeem Olajuwon. It lured you in with pork fat, faked you out with sugar, bounced you with garlic, elbowed you with peppercorns, and, just when you thought it was safe, laid it over your head with a touch of anise. But like the old Taco Bell commercials with Shaq and Hakeem arguing about crunchy or soft tacos, the answer is the double decker taco.

"Well, look, in terms of texture, I think they got me. And I haven't seen vinegar used in red-cooking that well since I last had Second Aunt's *ti pang,* but you're right. It's missing layers. I'm definitely going to tighten up our braising liquid, though, and experiment with vinegar. I like the viscosity in theirs."

Maybe in Evan's mind I make a more layered version of red-cooked pork, but I bow in the presence of greatness. To be this consistent, this good, and preserve your identity the way Old Jesse has is something I can only hope to be a part of. Dinner inspired me, but something about the restaurant told me I'd missed it. Old Jesse belonged to a bygone era.

It made me think of my dad. Not just 'cause Pops and Old Jesse are both dusty, but because eating at Old Jesse gave me the same feeling as playing my dad in the driveway. He never let me win. When I turned fifteen, I should have beat him—I was big enough and skilled enough—but I couldn't.

He always beat me with a running hook shot across the lane or a turn-around on the left block. I emulated a lot about my pops, but never that disgusting over-the-head Bill Cartwright jumper he had. So when I played him, I went on the block. I hit him with the heee and I hit him with the haaa, but every time it got to game point, he'd grab me, push me, and hold me if it meant winning.

"Yo, you can't hack me like that."

"Who says?"

"That's flagrant, man. You just grabbed my arm when I went to shoot."

"So? I'm not going to just let you beat me."

"I don't want you to let me beat you, but you have to play fair."

"I am play fair. I am allowed to foul."

"Whatever, man, check."

And every time I'd go back on the block, there he was again.

"WHAP!"

"What's wrong with you, man, just play defense."

"This is my defense! If you don't like it, don't play."

I didn't understand. I would never hack my dad on purpose. If he scored on me, he scored on me fair and square, I'd let him finish. I defended as much as I could within the rules but lived with the results. But he never let me get to my spots on the floor, he fouled as much as he could because there were no limits on fouls in the driveway, and he used everything he had to his advantage. Eventually, I'd attempt a move spinning around the baseline, ducking up and under to avoid contact, and clank it. He'd of course get the ball back and go to work. Patiently feeling me out nine feet from the hoop, faking one way, then running the other, creating just enough separation to release his hook shot off the glass.

"It's so cheap, you always go glass!"

"Glass is here, I'm allowed to use. If you don't like it, use yourself."

"You know this backboard is cheap and deads anything you throw at it."

"If you smart, you use the glass, too."

"I don't use the glass because I'm trying to work on my shot, if I just throw it at the glass I'm gonna have an ugly-ass Bill Cartwright jumper like you."

"Who cares? I'm not going NBA. And I just beat you. HA HA, SUCKER!"

Up until I was eighteen, he still beat me. Every single time, two or three times a week, I went out there to get hacked. I was determined to beat him without being cheap, but one day, he pissed me off. I was driving to the hoop on the right baseline by the bushes and he pushed me. My foot caught the gap between the concrete and the bushes. As I came down after my shot, I tweaked my ankle and fell.

"What the fuck is wrong with you, man? You almost sprained my ankle."

"You need to control yourself. There is no room to drive on the baseline."

After that, I changed. I realized that if I respected and yielded to—and emulated—my father forever, I'd never be myself. I had to beat him if he was ever going to let me go. I took the ball at the top of the key and gave up playing his game on the block. I exposed his biggest weakness: speed. I drove down the right side, time after time, forearm out, pushing off his chest to lay it in over his head.

"That's a push off!" he said.

"Call it, then."

To his credit, he never called it. He just shifted his stance and dared me to go left. In those days I couldn't go as fast left, so I darted left just to spin back right and shoot a turnaround. It worked for a few possessions, but he caught on and played the spin, catching me on my way back. I tried to go right again, but he was ready. He was going to make me earn my last few buckets in his office on the block.

Anticipating his foul on my drop step, I dropped, fake spun, elbowed him in the chest, then laid it in rolling into the lane.

"Take it easy! You just hit me in the chest," he complained.

"Game point."

I already knew what I was going to do. Twice now, I had spun and faked. He was going to play me for the fake so I went right to my move. Like Charles Barkley at the first hash, I dribbled for a good twenty seconds backing my dad down.

"Come on, man! You dribble forever."

"Shut up!"

I drop-stepped, hooked him with my off arm, then reverse laid it in.

"GAME. I win!"

I'd never been that upset at my dad. I walked off, left him, left the court, left the ball, and went inside where my mom was in the kitchen.

"Hey! How was the game?"

"AWESOME."

"Oh yeah?"

Before I could respond, in barreled my dad.

"No sportsmanship! You should be ashamed of yourself."

"Hey! What happened? Eddie say you had good game."

"Yeah, right! Good game. He has no sportsmanship. Sore loser."

"I'm not a sore loser. I won!"

"Eddie, calm down. What happened?"

"This son of bitch elbow me, then push me, then leave ball on floor after the game. You're the worst man. Who want to play with you anymore?"

"Eddie! You can't do that to your dad, he is older. You need to take it easy on him. You are going to hurt him."

"Every time I play, he scratches my arms and fouls me. He pushed me into the bushes today."

"Ay-yah, that's just how your dad is. You have to let him win, though."

"No, I don't! He has bad sportsmanship. I had to teach him a lesson."

"How, by being a bad sportsmanship, too?"

"Yeah!"

"No, Eddie. You are wrong. You can't just beat your dad. You have to beat him better."

"Why? He is a cheater!"

"Your dad is not a cheater, Eddie. He is testing you. If you can't beat him the right way, he can't let you go."

One of the most important things I learned in our Chinese home was to respect my elders. Yet, I didn't understand the breadth of this until I beat my dad fair and square. They may ask us to bow, but it's temporary. We earn the right to hold our heads high in the presence of our elders because it's not enough to be equals. We can't walk backward, and we can't move laterally. We have to transcend it. Just like I had to go through my dad and Michael had to go through Isiah, and LeBron had to go through Duncan, this generation of cooks has to go through the Old Jesses of the world.

The elders will scratch and claw and erect Bill Laimbeer like white walls in front of you, because they want to survive. Nothing wants to be the past. But before our fathers cede their thrones, they have to see us leap over their walls and empathize with their fear of the unknown. We don't know the future; they don't know what it means to fall into the past.

I understand my father. He wasn't ready to give up the driveway, but it didn't matter. I had to take it off him.

Xiao Zhen

Back in Chengdu, I still couldn't read the signs and symbols.

For three days, Emery, Evan (when he wasn't working on the taxes), and I wandered around Chengdu looking for things to do. We walked Jinli Lao Jie (Jinli Old Street) to try traditional Sichuan street foods and quickly realized it was a tourist trap serving outdated, but still delicious, renditions of dan-dan noodles and *san da pao* (three big cannons), glutinous rice balls ceremoniously thrown against a reverberating tray full of sesame and toasted soy.

Emery wanted to zone out at a twenty-four-hour spa theme park called Noah's Ark, so we trekked twenty-five minutes outside the city and lamped for about $50 apiece, meals included. We walked into what looked like a giant beige savings bank–themed casino, except the crowd was decidedly Chinese Outback Steakhouse. It made some sense to me that Chinese people would model a casino after a bank, since our idea of heaven, or at least vacation, is a Chase Bank with a super buffet. There were attractive women dressed like flight attendants greeting you as you walked in, but killing the Admiral's Lounge vibe were kids and parents pushing and shoving against your calves with rubber flotation devices on their arms racing to get to the exquisite-looking registration desk. I wasn't sure if I was applying for a loan at Wet 'n Wild or getting a locker at Noah's Ark, but I was intrigued.

The ideas of separation and elevation are relatively futile in China. The entire country is the Meadowlands. No matter how far up the ladder you climb, anyone short of the owner is still going to take the same shitty escalator to the same shitty bus to the same shitty PATH Train next to the same shitty person from Hoboken who's definitely going to puke on your shitty jeans. In China, even when you pay for the upgraded amenities, you can still see, hear, and smell the people in the upper deck farting *siu mai*, which I liked. No matter how much you try to ascend social strata in China, you're still anchored by the scent of egg wrappers and steamed pork wafting out of some Chinaman's ass while you try to find a good seat in the sauna.

At Noah's Ark, I thought about these things in the one pool without lane dividers, filled with young couples making out, families teaching their toddlers how to swim, and the ABC from New York trying to get his Michael Phelps on and swim laps. Initially, it seemed chaotic and impossible, but it worked. Of course, I couldn't swim my laps in one linear fashion, but only by winding my way around the various enclaves in the pool. Still, I got it in and came out the pool just as swole as I would at the New York Health and Racquet Club, i.e., not very swole at all but that's beside the point. You don't need to privatize the pool for linear consumption. It is extremely possible to have a multi-use pool that everyone can get busy in.

The scene was similar at IKEA. At the Chengdu IKEA, you'll see people conducting meetings in the office furniture displays where you get free refills of coffee. Instead of getting a room at Hakka Homes, people will go on dates at IKEA and lounge in the bedding section. Grandpa may just show up and fall asleep in the La-Z-Boy on a Sunday afternoon reading *People's Daily*. There's no shame in anyone's game in Chengdu. Luxury isn't a lifestyle; it's just a category of things. They seem to understand better than we do that none of it matters. A bag looks better with a logo and a meeting is more productive with coffee, but whether it's fake, real, or paid-for really doesn't matter. Expectations and self-awareness in this arena are just social constructs hailing from some fantastically nonsensical place beyond Tibet.

While Emery and Evan ran around Noah's Ark raiding the buffet for unlimited duck wings, I sat in the locker room. The chaos of Noah's Ark centered me, and in my moment of clarity, I pondered calling Dena's dad,

Mr. Fusco. Over the last two weeks, I'd told Evan, Emery, my parents, and my best friends about my plans to propose. And without fail, before I got off the phone, every one of them asked, "You gonna call her dad?"

My mind had skipped a few steps, and by this point I was assuming victory, assuming acceptance of the ring, and already moving on to setting aside part of the wedding budget for a Cam'ron appearance. I'd spent so much time thinking about how I was going to break the news to my mom and then convince Cam'ron to perform at the wedding that I hadn't thought of Dena's dad, but here I was. Ten days out from Dena's arrival in Chengdu, and I still hadn't told her pops. I didn't necessarily agree with the idea that you had to call someone's parents. Dena wasn't his property, and it seemed archaic, even excessively patriarchal, that you had to ask a father's permission to marry his daughter, but the traditionalist in me told me to do it. It was the right thing to do. Regardless, I was a little shook.

No matter how friendly a white person is to me, I'm still suspicious. I just assume they're going to find something in my life they don't understand and disown me. Dena understood this insecurity and force-fed herself my culture whenever she could. Even if she never actually finished any of her Rosetta Stone lessons, she tried. I wasn't sure if she was genuinely into it all, but I appreciated the effort; it's all I could ask. But how would Mr. Fusco receive me?

Whenever I met Dena's family, I tried to slowly reveal the secret of my Taiwanese-Chinese identity. I spent most of my time with her family focused on things we had in common: football, basketball, and, uhhh, hard work. We all like hard work? Yes, yes, and calamari? We like calamari. White cake is good? OK. Great. Do you like fruit in between the layers of white cake? No? OK, so, yeah, I hate it, too! What kind of human being puts nectarines, grapes, lychees, and strawberries in between a perfectly fine white cake? If the white cake wanted fruits in its personal space, it would have invited them! Yes, I agree, I hate fruit in my white cake as well! They are fucking trespassers!

The first time I visited Scranton with Dena, she had a dentist appointment. I sat in the waiting room watching their local news, amazed at the provinciality of it all, when the dentist came out.

"Hi, are you Eddie?"

"Yeah, nice to meet you."

He pulled his mask down, revealing his face, and shook my hand.

"I don't mean to make this awkward, but I am so excited to meet you."

"Oh, thanks, man."

"We got a group of guys, the Y-Pals, we work out together every morning, and Frank is always bragging about all the things you're doing like the restaurant, the shows, it's really cool stuff. I know he's excited to meet you this weekend."

"I'm excited to get to know him, too," I responded.

Dena walked back from the bathroom into her chair, so he put his mask back on and walked in.

"Anyway, see you soon, pal!"

I was flattered. I mean, how else can you feel? Your girlfriend's dad is excited to meet you. That's a good thing, right? I wasn't necessarily sure, but it stuck with me.

That night, Dena had a rehearsal with a group she used to sing with in town. She didn't really want to go, but her parents kept pressuring her, so she did it. While she was out, Mr. Fusco took me to a high school football game. Dena and I had only been dating about four months at the time, but without any fear or hesitation or time to get a hot dog, he got right into it.

"Ya know, Eddie, I just want Dena to be happy, but for her to be happy she needs direction. She is so talented, has so many ideas, but she just needs to pick something and go."

"I agree. I always told people in college that declaring a major is ceremonial. It's like going to LensCrafters. They're all just lenses to see the world from, and they're all going to do the same thing. You plug in your particular prescription and just go." I had a whole gang of digestible metaphors for parents I'd developed from my interactions with probation officers and college administrators.

"Exactly, Eddie! Exactly! And there's time in life for everything, but you have to start somewhere. . . . Have you heard her sing, Eddie?"

"No, not yet. She doesn't want to sing these days. I even took her to karaoke and she wouldn't do it, ha ha."

"Aw, geez. Geez Louise. Eddie, I don't know what to tell ya. She has the most beautiful voice. You gotta have her sing for you."

At the time, I thought of making an analogy between Dena's unwillingness to sing and the female orgasm, but luckily, something, a fleeting moment of integrity, maybe, stopped me.

"Well, I feel like you can't force it. The more you force it, the more she'll run, so I'm just going to pretend like I don't even know she has a voice." Or a clitoris.

"Eddie, I'm telling you, even if it's not her career, she should sing. She loves it and she's great. She's not going to be happy if she's not doing what she loves and that girl *loves* to sing."

I've met a lot of parents who think their kids are the best, but by the time they're twelve or thirteen things like soccer, algebra, or *American Idol* reinforce the possibility of their child's mediocrity. But Mr. Fusco deep down still felt Dena was the best. I didn't disagree.

In regard to his daughter, Mr. Fusco came to play forty-eight minutes plus double OT and expected me to as well. It was something I wasn't necessarily conscious of before, but as the time for my proposal drew closer, I realized that your girl's parents are inevitably going to be part of your relationship. You can get yourself through the first date, the first year, and so on, but when you start to see yourselves as a unit, as a family, inevitably the parents are part of the relationship. You can't deny it. You're a fool to think you're just marrying the person. Does anyone sell one fucking dinner fork? No! It doesn't make sense. Who buys one fork? Bank robbers and college kids at Surprise Surprise,* that's who, 'cause they have no intention of having families, but for the rest of us, you buy

---

* A place in the East Village that used to sell TERRIBLE home furnishings to NYU students.

the set. You have dinner for four, dinner for five, and when you're finally ready to call yourself a family, you buy a lazy Susan.

I tried to imagine going to the Fusco house during winter holiday for the next fifty years, and I wasn't mad at the visions. They had a nice-sized pool to swim laps in without couples making out. Mr. Fusco had the ill Notre Dame mancave in the basement to watch games, and if I wasn't going to have Chinese or Korean food on the couch, Italian and Jamaican would probably be the ones fighting it out for third place. Plus, they weren't just cooking "Italian" food.

These Northeast Pennsylvania Fuscos pulled out all the stops. Gravy fortified with meatballs, homemade sausage, and braciole; handmade manicotti, Mrs. Fusco's specialty; and stuffed clams. When we weren't eating in the home, they'd take us to Old Forge, 'cause it's not Old Forge pizza if you're not in the Pizza Capital of the World. Dena's brother, Joey, had a good head on his shoulders for fantasy sports, Mr. Fusco and I could agree to hate Ohio State the day after Thanksgiving, and Mrs. Fusco* was very curious about graffiti so I could always burn time with that. What else do you need in a biannual three-day trip to your future in-laws' house? I enjoyed visiting them because if you grew up in America, visiting Scranton feels like going home.

It was never my home, but this 1980s red-sauce image of family is what got projected into my consciousness. Scranton was everything I understood to be normal. Families like mine never watched *A Christmas Story* or *It's a Wonderful Life* at home—but if you slept over at your "normal" white friend's house you saw these movies. I'd talk about it when I got home and in an effort to expose us to more American culture, my mom took us to Pizza Hut. I guess it was our P. F. Chang's: something for foreigners to gaze on and eat appropriated victuals in an epic racialized setting.

---

* Mrs. Fusco is an art teacher and, being in Scranton, knows she's missing out on a lot of what's going on in art currently but stays really curious about street art and graffiti, constantly going into the city to see what's going on.

I remember reading books in elementary school to get coupons for free personal pan pizzas at Pizza Hut just so we could sit at a table with a checkered cloth and buy rubber NCAA Final Four basketballs. To us, it felt like we were sitting in a real Italian house. We were supposedly eating Italian food. They had cheese on the table! I didn't see cheese until my mom bought those little cow's head squares in middle school. And like Long Island Jews eating kosher Mongolian beef, we thought we were really doing it right for an hour. Although a lot of Italian and Jewish people have assimilated and disconnected from their roots, a couple generations back they were just like us, segregated to a small corner of town, working in the service industry, doing everything they could to maintain their identities. A hundred and fifty years later, what do we remember about Italian Americans besides meatballs and gangster flicks? *Vaffanculo!*

Eventually, urban sprawl is going to destroy everything. As Scranton's own Jane Jacobs* has shown us, project stairwells, Central Park, and Walmarts are the bane of our existence. But before their culture died in a mini-mall, I wondered, did O.G. white people back in the fifties and sixties go to the Scranton YMCA trying to swim laps, but had to zig-zag around Italians making out, Italians flapping arms, and Italians causing traffic jams? Because in the eyes of this Taiwanese-American Chinaman, Scranton is just as exotic and spectacular as Chengdu. Everybody poops, everybody dies, and one day everybody's home gets resurrected as mise-en-scène. This could be my home, too, right? I wasn't sure about all this, but I kept recontextualizing Dena and her family because I didn't want to make the mistake of seeing them as the other. I loved her and, somehow, I had to find a way to love her family. I just needed to understand them first.

Sitting there in the locker room at Noah's Ark, I bit the bullet and

---

* Jane Jacobs wrote the seminal book *The Death and Life of Great American Cities*, which explained why the garden city and urban sprawl would lead to the demise of our cities, which are much more efficient, sustainable, and safe ways to organize society.

called Mr. Fusco. My heart rate was on ten like I just took a dab* as the phone rang. By the third ring, I thought about hanging up, but then I heard a click. I was on.

"Hey! Mr. Fusco, how's it going?"

"I'm great, Eddie, I'm great. How are you? How's China?"

"It's great, it's great. It's, uhhh, China!"

"Great. Well, that's great. I'm glad you called."

"Oh yeah? That's great." We were the Two Stooges having a "great" contest.

"Yeah, yeah, you know, Dena told me she was going to China, and I wanted to talk to you about it."

By now, I was wild nervous. Palms sweating, eyes darting, heart raging, mind racing trying to figure how I was going to ask him if he was cool with me proposing to his daughter.

"Great, great, yeah, let's talk about China!"

"Well, where are you all staying?"

Fuck. I never thought about what Mr. Fusco would say if he realized we were staying at a by-the-hour hotel in southwestern China.

"Oh, we're staying at this GREAT place, Hakka Homes, lots of students, young people, it's a real community at Hakka Homes."

"Great. Great. Because ya know, Eddie, this idea of Dena in China, I'm just not that excited about it. I tell ya, I have to be honest, I'm not excited at all about it."

I hadn't even gotten to the proposal part, and he was already uncomfortable with her just visiting me in China.

"OK, uhhh, well, that's not good. That's not good. What makes you not excited about it?"

"Listen, it's just a movie, but have you ever seen *The Firm*?"

"The Tom Cruise movie?"

"Yup. Yup. That one, Eddie, *The Firm*. . . . It was on last night, and I gotta tell ya, it doesn't have me very excited about my daughter in China."

---

*   Freebasing weed in wax form.

I'd never seen *The Firm*, but I remember the cover had Tom Cruise in a suit running from something while holding a briefcase, so I just went with it. I guess Mr. Fusco was worried Dena would be running in a suit with a briefcase in China?

"Well, I'm here in China and my family is Chinese and it's not as bad as Tom Cruise makes it out to be."

"But, Eddie, it's a communist country and, look, you know I'm an open-minded guy, but come on. You've seen *The Firm*. . . . I don't have to tell you how bad it can get. It's not the same. It's not America."*

I accepted that Mr. Fusco was nervous. I understood that these propagandistic, xenophobic visions of China represented the entirety of most of America's knowledge of China. I respected that he was telling me exactly why he was tight, because some other parent with liberal guilt probably would have withheld the communist part of the commentary, only to channel those feelings into something like lead-based paint or bird flu, but I was pissed. There were a million reasons for me to not like Scranton, but I never mentioned the fucking *Exorcist*!† Also, how can you be proud of everything I do in *your* country, brag to the dentist, but be diametrically opposed to the country and culture my ancestors are from without ever understanding it? Regardless, I was committed to getting off the phone gracefully, but not without trolling him a bit.

"Well, Mr. Fusco, I can tell you that I specifically picked Hakka Homes because it's only two blocks from the United States Embassy."

"Get outta here! Two blocks? That's great, Eddie. That's terrific."

"Yup, two blocks to freedom, no big deal, anything happens, we run with the briefcase down the hall like Tom Cruise and we're at the embassy."

"Oh, geez, Eddie, don't say that, ha ha. God forbid, but that's good you're near the embassy. That's great."

"All right, well, I'll pick up Dena at the airport when she comes.

---

* To this day I have not seen *The Firm*, but my editor assures me it has nothing to do with China. To this day I also have no idea what the fuck Mr. Fusco was talking about.

† Jason Miller, who played Father Karras in *The Exorcist*, is from Scranton.

We'll call you immediately and maybe we'll even get you a photo of us in front of the embassy."

"Awesome. All right, thanks, Eddie. Listen, I just want to make sure my baby is OK, so it's good to hear from you, big guy. I'm glad you're doing well. What do you think about the Wolverines this year?"

"I like Gardner. I think he's athletic, but he can actually throw the ball. Shoelace was a third-down slash QB that they tried to make a full-time starter. He should have been Percy Harvin, not Tim Tebow."

"I agree, I agree, Eddie, gotta be able to throw the ball these days. All right, well, you have fun, and we'll talk soon."

"Take care, Mr. Fusco!"

I hung up the phone, headed to the spa's movie theater, and tried again not to judge parents until I'd been one myself.

Noah's Ark sprawled on and on. Beyond the super buffet, pool, hot tubs, and saunas, there were a movie theater, racquetball courts, arcade games, La-Z-Boys with satellite television, and massage rooms. Evan and Emery had been watching a movie, so I sat outside on the steps until they finished.

"How was the movie?"

"Eh, we fell asleep," Emery said.

"Sound system was good, though. They just play action films to show off the surround sound," Evan said.

"So it's like watching a movie in the backseat of a college drug dealer's ES 300?"

"LOL. Pretty much like your old car but with foreign films," Emery said. And he really did say "LOL."

"What you guys wanna do now?"

Before they could answer, two early-twentysomething girls walked over in a different uniform than the others.

"*Ni hao, shui gu!*"*

---

* "Hello, handsome brother!" is a common greeting in service-industry China.

"*Ni hao, ni hao,*" Emery responded.

"Hmmm, what is this, dope spice?" said Evan.*

"Would you guys like a massage?"†

Emery looked around excitedly.

"Yes! Yes, I would like a massage. How do we do this?" he said.

"Well, we have many price ranges depending on how long you want the massage for. We also have many nutritious healthy benefits, treatments, and oils if you like."

"Eddie, this is a medical expense. I'm pretty sure you can write this off."

"Evan, if I get us all massages, will you push through and knock out the 2011 taxes for Baohaus tomorrow?"

"Man, I'm trying! You can't just give me half of Baohaus or buy me a massage and expect the taxes to be done miraculously. It takes time."

"I could give a lot of people half of Baohaus and they would definitely do the tax audit."

"I kind of agree with Eddie, Evan. The value of what Eddie gives you is definitely worth dealing with the tax audit. Plus, he paid for us all to come out to China. You need to finish the taxes."

"Fuck you guys. Emery, you worked with Eddie, too. He does all the 'fun' shit and we get stuck with the paperwork."

"That's your choice, Evan. You could go open your own restaurant, but this is Eddie's restaurant. He put up the money, he made the food, he created the brand, he's the one responsible when Sam Sifton doesn't like it, and you're responsible for the taxes!"

"Thank you, Emery. And the taxes are due in October, Evan. Get it done."

---

* We started calling things dope spices that year because the homie Benny Blanco told Emile that he made this "dope soup" and we were like, "What's in this dope soup?" and he couldn't say. When we pressed him on it, he says, "I don't know, man! Like fucking dope spices." So the recipe for Benny Blanco's dope soup is, of course, dope spices. Don't tell anyone....

† The girls spoke no English, but all of the dialogue has been translated so that you don't have to look down at footnotes every sentence.

"IT'S JULY!"

Instead of reminding him once again that the taxes were already over-due, already being audited, and on an extension, I bit my tongue and thought about how nice a massage would be. There's nothing better than a straight-up medicinal massage in China. Chinese masseurs find muscles you didn't know you had, eviscerate old scar tissue, pop your ankles, cure old basketball injuries, and leave you smelling like the illest stripper this side of Jamaica, Queens. I'm pretty sure they can fix anything short of LeBron's toes.* While most men in the U.S. can't say "massage" without daydreams of happy endings, massage in East Asia actually stands at the intersection of art, culture, and medicine. There are your $10 boardwalk gypsies practicing the craft badly, your $50 red-light-district hot-towel extraordinaire, and the $100 top-of-the-mall lifestyle massage practitioner where you bring clients instead of taking them on a golf outing. But my favorite version is the medicinal massage.

The best massage I ever received was in Kentin, Taiwan, a beach town with a massage parlor set up like Katz's Deli, flooded with bright halogen lights. If you were drunk after a night of karaoke, you'd grab a few grilled squid sticks outside and stumble in for the world's best medicinal massage. That night, I walked in with an old shoulder injury from fighting Emery, a chronic sprained ankle from basketball, and giant welts on my back from falling on rocks surfing. Two out of three were injuries I'd seen doctors for and paid deductibles on without any progress or resolution. Without any real expectation of solving my problems, I lay down on the cot that should have had a sign demarcating that Meg Ryan once sat there.†

"What kind of problems you got, kid?" screamed the old woman in a dishwasher's shirt with a cigarette hanging out of her mouth.

"I hit some rocks surfing and my back hurts."

"OK, flip over, face down, let me take a look."

---

*   Google LeBron's feet. RIP toes. . . .

†   At Katz's, there's a sign pointing down at the table Meg Ryan sat in for *When Harry Met Sally*.

She poked and prodded my lats, felt the welts, and then ran her fingers over my spine.

"You have old injury! Disc is crooked."

"How do you know that without taking an MRI?"

"Ha! MRI. I use MY HANDS. Anyone can tell you have herniated disc."

Just as I started to respond, she shut me down.

"Stop talking! I'm checking the rest of you out. I don't need any more description from you leaving out all the good information! I use my hands and figure this out myself." She laughed.

For the next five minutes, I just lay there like a stupid piece of bologna trying to hide its olives and peppers.

"Labrum has scar tissue.

"Ankle dislocated before.

"Stomach is out of place. You must have puked recently."

As she moved around my stomach, I thought the next comment was going to be "Your FUPA is crooked." But luckily she spared any commentary on my fat upper pussy area.

"OK, give me your arm. Bend your elbow and stay loose."

I tried to follow her instructions as best as I could but failed miserably.

"Eh! Eh, I told you to stay loose. How am I going to fix this if you're stiff? Let me rotate your arm. If you keep being stiff, then I have to use more force."

Quickly, I told myself to make like badly cooked glass noodles and let loose.

"There you go. OK, stay loose, I'm going to put this muscle back on track."

There was a hot sensation, followed by a crack in my shoulder like the sound of a bike chain catching onto a new gear, and then an explosion of relief like the last day of school.

"What the fuck did you just do?"

"I fixed you! Gimme a second, then I fix the rest of you," she said as she lit a new cigarette.

For forty-five minutes, she worked her way around, listening to my body and exorcising it like the scar tissue whisperer. The constant shifting between acute pain and physical release was confounding. She hovered over me, plucking the fibers of my muscles, flicking the crevices of the bones, bringing peace to the region of my spine that had been warring with my hamstrings for years. When she was done, I lay there buzzing with blood rushing through my fascia in steam-table purgatory like a giant side of beef set aside for resurrection as a Reuben sandwich in the "world to come." But before I was allowed to pass into the next realm, someone shook me back to this life.

"Do you want a spa massage, too?" the Noah's Ark girl asked me.

I looked up at her and blinked.

"Hey! Hello? Sir! Do you want a massage? Your brothers already left," she said as I stood there in the middle of my Kentin day trip.

"Oh, hey, my bad. Wait, my brothers already went?"

"Ha ha, yes, they are doing massage."

I really wasn't into spa massage because there were no real benefits. Most of these girls don't know how to cure a side of beef with the art of *tui na*,* so you're paying for a terrible hour-long facedown fake date with a Chinese girl from a rural town where she humors you about how charming you are as she haphazardly elbows at vertebrae. Then again, the conversational massage is better than a shitty real date that involves an entire meal of food and eye contact. Plus, I hadn't seen my girl in a month.

"I'll do the massage."

"Great! Come this way, *shui gu!*"

We arrived at the room, and I lay facedown into the table without saying too much, my mind still considering Mr. Fusco and his interpretation of China. What is it that kids do to people? In all other facets, Mr. Fusco was seemingly liberal, open-minded about others, albeit conservative in his own business, but with Dena he was an autocrat. I tried not to take his comments about China and communism personally, but they had me bugged out.

"Where are you from?" asked the massage girl.

_____

* Chinese massage technique, literally "push-pull."

"New York," I answered, trying not to engage as I stayed in my head thinking about the Fuscos.

"Wow! Big city. I always want to go."

"Chengdu is a big city, too."

"Yes, but America different. It just seems so . . . easy, relaxed."

Her insistence caught me off guard.

"How so?"

"It just seems magical, romantic, and easier. China is so hard."

"Ha ha, I can't relate. I understand you, but I can't relate."

"Why not?"

"Because I live there. Every person, every city, every country has its own struggle. We just have better marketing."

"I don't think so. . . . How much do you make?"

"You really want to know?"

"It's not hard to see, *da gu*. You just look expensive," she said, laughing.

"I'll probably do three hundred fifty K before taxes and commission this year so, take-home a hundred and fifty K."

"WOW! What do you do?"

"I write books, cook food, host some shows."

"You must have a girlfriend, don't you?"

"Yeah, I do."

"*Wa sai*,* I figure you would have a girlfriend because you are cute in a chubby big brother way, but now when you talk about money . . . You must have MANY girlfriends."

"Ha ha, it's not like that. I just got one."

"Chinese girl?"

"Irish-Italian."

"*WA SAI!* You really have kung fu. That is not easy."

"Usually the other way around, right?"

"Exactly. American men come here and love us, but white women *bu shuai ya zhou nan ren*."†

---

* Wow.

† Don't give two fucks about Chinese men.

"What's your name?"

"Xiao Zhen. You are Xiao Ming!"

"How do you know?"

"I heard your brothers talking to you. We were watching you three running around earlier."

"Why's that?"

"You guys look interesting. Definitely not from here, but also not like other American Chinese. You seem bad!"

"Bad? Why bad?"

"Not baaad, but like bad boy. Very exciting to girls, you know."

She laughed. I liked her, even though I knew she was at least partially gassing me.

"I guess."

"Let me see photo of your girlfriend."

I pulled up my phone and showed her a photo of Dena and me goofing off on a sidewalk on the Lower East Side of Manhattan. Dena was wearing a leather jacket and Ray-Bans, with a Based FOB hat perched on her head.

"Oh! You must be a good person. Your girlfriend is very nice. You can tell a lot about a person by their girlfriend."

"You can."

"How did you meet?"

"I gave her drugs at a bar."

"Ay-yah! You *are* a bad person."

"She asked for it!"

"You are not bad person, you just troublemaker, but it's cute. What is she like?"

"She's my best friend. I know it's what everyone says, but she's really just my best friend. I can't explain why, I'm just comfortable with her. We fit."

"That's the most important. Everything goes away except friendship and family."

"Yeah, must be hard in China. No one has brothers and sisters."

"I have a sister!"

"I thought you could only have one in China?"

"Yes, but in rural area like I'm from families can have more than one. I just came to Chengdu to make money and send home."

"So how much do you make?"

"I will make you cry!"

"How much?"

"I work twenty-eight days out of every month in these stupid heels and take home forty-five hundred RMB."*

"Cot damn. . . . So when I tell you that 'everyone has their own struggle,' you'd still say it's harder in China?"

"Absolutely. America is easier. China is growing, changing, people at top making money, but very very hard for the rest of us. We all want a better life, but we don't know if this is better."

"I don't know what to tell you. I definitely prefer drinking water in America, living in America, working in America, but seeing what I saw growing up, I feel like you get further and further away from what makes you happy, the more you chase it. I know many Chinese people that come to America because it's a 'better life,' but in their old age go home. Home is always home."

"I agree. Being daughter of farmer, it is easier back home but everything around you changes and you have no choice but to join in. China, you know, had very tough last hundred years. Right now, China needs all of us to pitch in and catch up, but it is very hard on the little people."

"Do you have a boyfriend?"

"No, I don't."

"You massage dudes all day, you don't find any you like?" I joked.

She slapped my back.

"See! Bad boy! So mean! I don't have time for dating. I have friends here, but we are all working."

"What do you do when you're not working?"

"*Da gu*, when am I not working?"

---

* $728.

"What's your schedule?"

"We come in at twelve P.M. and leave at midnight twenty-eight days a month. I live at Noah's Ark!"

"How long does it take you to get home?"

"No, you don't understand. *I live at Noah's Ark.*"

"You live here?"

"Yeah, the building next to Noah's Ark is to house employees. Most of us work here because we can send all the money home. We get housing, food, uniforms; most money can go home."

"What does your sister do?"

"Same thing. My parents are getting old, and we want to save up enough money to keep our house."

"*Wa sai. . . .*"

"Ahhh, don't sweat it, *da gu,* not your fault."

"I'm lucky I was born in America, but it just shouldn't matter as much as it does."

"At least you can see it. Many Americans come and you can tell they can't see the difference."

"What do you mean by difference? My Chinese isn't that good."

"Your Chinese is fine. I mean the difference between you and me. We are both Chinese, but so much in between, so much changed because you were born in America. I have lots of things I want to do. I have dreams, too, but I will never get to see them happen because I am born here with the parents I have."

All this time, I was still facedown in the massage table unable to look at her face as she said these things. But I felt my eyes watering into the towel. Everything was wrong. I literally wanted to switch positions and give her a massage, but I couldn't. That's not what she wanted. I could have given her money, but it would have been insulting. I was engulfed in guilt, but instead of making it about myself, I got my shit together and remembered it was about her.

"You have to make time for yourself. No one will make you happy but yourself."

"Not true! Your girlfriend makes you very happy, doesn't she?"

"She makes me happy because she makes herself happy."

"Huh?"

"Yeah. I like her because she likes herself. She expects things for herself. She wants to do things for herself. She knows herself."

"That is very strange. Don't you want a woman that takes care of you? Why do you like her because she takes care of herself? She should already do that."

"She should, but a lot of girls don't take care of themselves. They take care of their families and boyfriends, but who takes care of them? My mom is like that. She spent her whole life taking care of my dad and the three of us but didn't take care of herself."

"I don't know. I think it is important that woman take care of man. You are exceptional person. Whoever your girlfriend is must know how to take care of you."

"She does. But if I wanted a maid or a nurse, I'd get one. I want a partner."

"Wow. You are a very rare man. . . . I never hear a man say these things. Your girlfriend is very lucky," she said again as she rearranged my towel.

What she was saying was nice, but accepting compliments like this is what got Caesar killed. First, I didn't think it was rare. Second, it was just game, right? It's her job to massage lumpy pear-shaped men and act like it's Tyrese Gibson lying there! I wasn't trying to be another Captain Kirk swooping some destitute Chinese working woman off her feet, nor was I trying to get a cheap bucket on the slide. Then again, why was I trying to fit this exchange into some kind of category? She was a person! A person I had a real connection with even if it started in a fucked up indentured servitude setting.

I kept telling myself: "She's not a massage girl; she's a person who massages." And what's wrong with a person who massages? She had more poignant things to say than anyone I'd met in Shanghai—all those upwardly mobile shitheads educated abroad returning home to embrace the "Chinese Dream" blind to the static and unforgiving lives of people who bear the burden for this country. Mobility is a fundamental right afforded to few.

This is the real reason, I realized, that I came to China—to stare my other life in the face. I had to know who I could have been if my parents had never immigrated to America.

Dena had to see it, too: who I could have been, who I may still be. Maybe deep inside I am a Little Red Book–carrying communist!

Not only did I need Dena to see me in the context of my ancestral homeland, I needed to know she understood it and accepted it. Sure, acceptance extinguished Bob Marley and sentenced him to college dorm room walls next to John Mayer, but this is a different kind of acceptance. The kind of acceptance that fulfills you; the kind of acceptance that emerges from revealing every layer to your better half until all that's left is a mangled, embryonic ego curled into the fetal position.

At that moment you're just a pus-colored mass of fear and insecurity bubbling on two plates. And bae still wraps you up, and takes you to-go. I didn't have to hide my secret identity any longer. It was time for Dena and Mr. Fusco to know.

Luckily all these thoughts were happening facedown. I collected my-self and redirected the conversation.

"I am actually going to propose to her when she comes to China."

"No way! Really? That is so exciting. Have you spoken to her father?"

"I tried about an hour ago, but he was weird."

"Did you ask?"

"I was going to, but he offended me. He started talking about how China is not safe and communist. It made me mad."

"Ahhh, Americans are just like this. They don't know their place. They are big brother but don't act like it. You shouldn't be mad at her dad."

"Yeah, but why should we let them constantly disrespect us? It's not OK to say these things. We Americans have it better in every way, and we have no shame. We don't realize all the advantages we have and how hard it is for everyone else, but we think it's OK to criticize everyone, go into their countries, and tell them how to do things. Even if we are better at some things, at least be gracious about it."

"People at the top have to remember the rest of us. All we want is a *chance* to be respected. Not even respect, but the opportunity to earn someone respect, you understand? We don't even have that. Most people come here and see we are powerless, so they try to grab our legs, touch our breasts, take advantage when they should be doing opposite. You already have everything, still want to come disrespect me? OK, flip over."

I flipped over, eyes red, lines from the towels all over my chest. I closed my eyes and hid the evidence.

"Do you sometimes want to date a Chinese girl?"

"No, but I think about it. I think about it a lot."

"Does your girlfriend understand us?"

"I think so. I hope so," I said and paused. I didn't actually know.

"She is always learning," I stammered. "I'm just glad she wants to. If she didn't genuinely want to understand us, I couldn't be with her."

"That's good. I just feel like you are a very special Chinese man, and I hope that she recognize this. It would be total waste if you have a wife that does not understand everything you are, especially being Chinese."

"Think of it this way. I am a privileged Chinese-Taiwanese-American kid who really wants to understand you. She is an Irish-Italian American who wants to understand me. There's a gap between all of us, right? Even though you tell me what it's like to work at Noah's Ark, I can't possibly understand it unless I do it."

"Right, I get that. But you want to. I'm just saying . . . make sure she wants to understand you. Women are tricky, and you really are a very special Chinese person."

"You don't have to flatter me. We're friends now."

"No, I know. I'm not saying it because you are a customer. You really are special. You shouldn't forget it. Not all of us get to be special."

Mr. Zheng

We took a cab home from Noah's Ark, and greeting us downstairs from Hakka Homes at 1 A.M. were two giant pots of crawfish boiling. Was this the new wave?

Usually, if you walked by a stall, the owner would bark you into buying an order, but crawfish homie just sat on his metal stool reading his newspaper and smoking his Hong He cigarette. Not only was he uninterested in selling crawfish, but he had a polo shirt covering his stomach and a haircut that you might have described as . . . flirty? I think son used pomade. By Chengdu standards, he could have been an i-banker if he hadn't been wearing shower sandals.

I walked up to the two pots of boiling crawfish and poked my head into the steam expecting it to melt my face with chili and peppercorn vapors, but all I got was aged rice wine. Strange. It didn't even have the dry mild heat of Old Bay or Zatarain's you'd see in a New Orleans boil.

If I had been to this spot my first week in Chengdu, it would have been a godsend. I spent hours that week trying to find food from someplace other than McDonald's or Hooters that wouldn't set my asshole on fire, but after two weeks my body adjusted. I didn't have diarrhea every day and I craved chilis. Not to torch my palate, but just to know it was there. Like the scent Dena left in the "Virgin Vagina"* T-shirt I subcon-

---

* She always wore this T-shirt to bed that said "Vagina" in that Virgin Airlines font. I brought it and even after a wash, it still smelled like her when I put it on.

sciously packed in my suitcase and took to Chengdu, chilis were there even when they weren't.

"What's up with these crawfish?" I asked in Mandarin.

"Forty RMB a kilo," said Crawfish Man as he folded his newspaper and stood up from the stool.

"You guys want crawfish?" I asked Emery and Evan.

"I'm tired, man. I'll see you tomorrow," said Evan.

"I'll hang. I'm not hungry but I'll try one," said Emery.

"All right. One kilo, please."

"OK."

Crawfish Man went to the pot closest to his stool and started scooping out a kilo of crustaceans.

"Do you have two different flavors in the pots?"

"Nope. One flavor. That pot is still soaking. This pot is ready to serve."

He came over with a Styrofoam plate and a plastic bag full of bright red crawfish topped with chopped scallions. Nothing else.

"You guys aren't from around here, are you?" he asked.

"Nah. I'm from New York, he's from Florida."

"Enjoy."

I put my face in the bag to smell the crawfish close up.

"How is it?" asked Emery in English.

"It smells more like *lu wei* than a crawfish boil. There's a lot of sweetness, like a five-spice stock."

Emery got closer to smell it.

"Weird. No pepper. No lemon. No cilantro, even."

I picked up the crawfish, twisted the head, slurped the guts, and squeezed the tail. For a second, I was confused. The taste was so clean, yet rustic, like braised yellow croaker. It was a simple concept. He'd taken EBT* lobster and turned down the muddiness, while accentuating its essence without overpowering the natural sweetness of the protein.

"Yo. . . . You're not from here, either," I said to him.

---

* Electronic Benefit Transfer . . . i.e., welfare lobster.

"Ha ha, why do you say?"

"This ain't no Chengdu crawfish."

"No, it's not. I'm from Shanghai."

"Ahhh, that's why you don't have your belly out."

He laughed, folded his newspaper, and pulled up a stool.

"Do you like it?" he asked.

"I do. I like it a lot."

"In Shanghai, this is how we do it. Milder, sweeter crawfish boil. But even in Shanghai now, many places use chilis and peppercorns. Sichuan cooking is very popular. I came here to bring Shanghai style to Sichuan."

"Doesn't Shanghai have better potential for business, though?" asked Emery.

"Not for food. Everybody in China knows. If you want to be known for food, you come to Chengdu. Here, they have *tze huo*."*

By now, my attention was being torn at the ends. I was so interested in the conversation, but my hands kept digging into the crawfish. When he brought up chowhounds in Chengdu, I was intrigued but also bugged out because I looked down and I was out of crawfish.

"Hey, no disrespect, boss. I definitely want to keep talking, but do you think I could get another kilo of crawfish?"

"Ha ha, no problem. I'm glad you like it. . . . You know my business is good, but Chengdu people just don't get it. Everyone comes and says they like it but that I should add chilis. I don't understand. If you like it, why do you change it? If I add chilis, then it's not Shanghainese flavor. Then what's the point?"

A couple days later, I stumbled home after karaoke and found Crawfish Zheng outside again.

"Hey! Mr. Zheng, how's it going?"

"You know, same old, same old. How are you, Xiao Ming?"

"I just killed it at karaoke."

"Oh yeah? You a good singer?"

---

*   Chowhounds.

"No, I'm more of a karaoke performer."

"Ha ha, OK, I understand."

"Lemme get two kilos of crawfish!"

"OK, no problem."

I handed him the money, and he tried to turn me down.

"Come on, lemme pay."

"No, no, you are a guest, it's on me."

"You are too kind. I'm a customer here."

Eventually, I left the money under a bowl of cilantro and dug into the crawfish. I really liked Mr. Zheng and I realized that I hadn't cooked *with* anyone in China yet. I'd been doing a lot of eating, a lot of talking, and a lot of thinking about Dena, but I'd forgotten to cook. Of course, I'd cooked at Hakka Bar and Evan helped me out, but I wanted to cook outside. With Mr. Zheng. I wasn't particularly sure what I was after but the idea met me with great certainty.

"Mr. Zheng, I was wondering. Do you think I could come cook with you one night?"

"You want to make crawfish?"

"No, I want to make Taiwanese beef noodle soup! It would go good with the crawfish."

"Ahhh, Taiwanese beef noodle soup! I love it. Very hard to find."

"Yeah, they got a lot of Sichuan beef noodle soup here, but they don't focus on the soup, it's flat and they just top it with chili oil."

"Exactly. Taiwanese food is great but hard to find in China."

"Yeah, I'll pay rent, too. Lemme know what day I can come."

"No rent, just come, Thursday night we'll have fun. Pay me in soup."

The next day, I went down to see if Mr. Zheng wanted to get lunch, but the grilled-skewer dude who was in his spot told me Zheng wouldn't be back till after ten.

Since I couldn't get lunch with Mr. Zheng, I went through my phone to see who was on WeChat. Emery and Evan were still asleep. Corky had apparently just gotten home from karaoke in Shanghai. And Hakka Heather was out of town. But there was Rabbi, the homie with the Fabolous tattoo. I messaged him.

Yo, Rabbi! You eat lunch yet?

Hey man! Wassup? No, not eat yet. You want to
come studio, bro?

Yeah, where's your studio? I'll take a cab.

No, no, no, I come pick you up. Be outside in ten minutes,
I have black car.

Chinese hospitality never ceased to amaze me. Whether it was Hakka
Heather, Corky, or Rabbi, they always insisted on picking me up and
fighting for the bill. None of them were wealthy by any means, at most
middle class, but as a guest in China, I wasn't allowed to pay for anything. I tried to repay them or give them things like books, hats, or liquor
I had brought with me to China, but later reversed strategy because anytime I gave them gifts, they went over the top and bought me one better.
You couldn't win with these Chinese people. I remember Corky said
that China was a country full of only children serviced by six adults, but
for me China felt like one giant country full of aunts and uncles picking
up the tab.

Rabbi picked me up in his car, which was definitely black, but in
New York when you say black car, you mean "Town Car or better." This
was a China-Russia-only brand ride.

"What kind of car is this? I've never seen it before."

"Some Russian shit, you don't get this in America. You got to be down
to get this limited edition Skoda, man," he said sarcastically.

"Skoda, huh? Kinda like a Volkswagen that wants to be an Alfa Romeo."

"More like rickshaw that wants to be Volkswagen! This made by same
company as Volkswagen, but Russian shit," said Rabbi.

I looked up Skoda on my phone.

"It says online that it's actually a Czech brand."

"Like I said, Russian shit," he said, laughing.

"Ha ha, a lot of Russian cars in China, huh?"

"Yeah, man, good stuff at good price. Russia is neighbors, so they come here buy fake leather shoes, fake fur coat, fake Apple stuffs, other Chinese fake shit. We buy the cars, sometimes they send the girls, sometimes we send the girls. It's cool. China-Russia always trading."

To date, that is still the best distillation of Russia-China relations I've ever heard.

Before I had a moment to think about it though, I noticed Rabbi's T-shirt. In the midst of all this faux goods talk, I realized Rabbi was wearing a "Don't Buy the Fake Shit!" tee.

"You know what ironic means, Rabbi?"

"Yeah, man, I read about this. Like when you say something but gives weird feeling because you do something kind of opposite you saying, right? Like hypocrites funny."

"Ha ha, yeah, you mad ironic because your shirt says 'Don't Buy the Fake Shit' but you're driving a bootleg Volkswagen."

"Yeah! That's sneakers, street wear, shit I like, I don't buy the fake shit. Other stuffs, car, computer, who cares, but things I care about like hip-hop culture, I buy the real. You got to support the culture, man. Things with no meaning, you buy the fake shit smart."

We got to his studio and parked the car downstairs. It was next to a parking garage and a bakery on a relatively busy neighborhood block in an area near Chengdu's colleges.

"So, see, this my studio."

It looked just like every skate shop office or college DJ dorm room I'd ever seen. Shit, it kinda looked like my apartment on East 12th Street in New York when I was selling sneakers and street wear.

Somehow, even without ever coming to America, but just being into the culture, Rabbi had channeled it perfectly. Everything was effortless and so fucking futuristically real. When you came in the door, he had leather house slippers. There was an electric flyswatter, a Japanese brand hot water heater for making tea, a small alcove kitchen, a beat-up futon couch for listening to beats or seducing some girl you told to come over and listen to beats. Then he had two turntables, some of the same stickers I had, some anime posters I didn't, records, computers, and cords everywhere. I'd been in so many places that felt like this but not with the Chengdu accents and chili-infused everything. Another vision of my possible double China life presented itself.

"You record here?"

"No, we make mixes, tapes, flyers, party stuff."

"Word, you DJ, huh?"

"Yeah, DJ Super Best Friend. That's me."

"What? Your name is DJ Super Best Friend?"

"For sure, that's cool, right?"

There was a pause, as I thought about whether my alternate universe name could have been DJ Super Best Friend. Possibly. I mean why not? It's nice! OK, no, my name would never be DJ Super Best Friend. My name might be DJ No New Friends or DJ Slap Your Super Best Friend or DJ Tanner or Uncle Jesse, but no, my name could not possibly be DJ Super Best Friend.

"Hey, Eddie. I gotta ask you. I see these T-shirts, too, they say 'Cool Story, Bro.' What's that mean?"

"If someone tells you a shitty story, then you respond ironically, 'Cool story, bro,' to their really not cool story."

"Cool story, bro," he said with a smile.

"Loser," I said as I pushed him.

I definitely could have been DJ Cool Story, Bro.

"What are you playing at these cool parties of yours?"

"Man, they make me play the wack shit sometimes."

"Who makes you play the wack shit?"

"The owner of Jellyfish, the club we throw party. Old Israeli guy he like-a the Pitbull, Katy Perry, super wack shit, bro."

"What do you want to play, though?"

"I know everything. From backpack rap like Boot Camp to Fabolous to new stuff like A$AP and Kendrick, I play it all. China is slow, we get everything late, but once we get it we take the time, pay attention, listen to everything."

"You don't have to wait. You can just download online with VPN, right?"

"Eddie, I don't even know where to search! I know the Chinese hip-hop sites, but they put up tapes months after already out in America."

"OK, lemme see your computer."

I took his computer, used his VPN, and took him to the vault.

"All right, this is going to solve your problem. Really easy, just go to datpiff.com and you get all the new mixtapes. You want to read news, go to nahright.com. You want more news, go to Noisey on Vice. You need more stuff, email me."

"Fuck! Cool, bro. This is awesome. What should I download?"

"Everyone playing Migos in the club right now. You should play that Chinatown shit and see what people think out here."

"They have a song called 'Chinatown'?"

"Yeah, it's dope."

"OK, downloading now."

We sat there looking at the download that went from five minutes, to eight minutes, to thirty minutes, to an hour, and just sat at 2 percent downloaded for a good ten minutes.

"Like I said, Eddie, not so easy. VPN get you on the site, but this never going to download."

It didn't seem like a big deal, but I saw Rabbi literally crumble. He put his head in his hands, closed up his laptop, and dragged his feet across the floor as he went to put the computer away.

"It's no big deal, man, just leave your computer open and it'll down-load."

"Eddie . . . even when you showing me, telling me it's easy, I already know this going to happen. You are not first American I've met tell me they can help me get songs. This is China, man, if they don't want us to see something, we not going to see it."

Rabbi's melodramatic response to the dream deferred of a Migos mix-tape aside, I was beginning to understand that being Chinese in Chengdu was like being a goldfish. You can see the outside world, you might be able to hear the outside world, but you can't touch it, at least not in real time. He took it really hard. Or maybe I was taking it too lightly. I wasn't sure I'd ever seen a world I couldn't touch.

We got back in the Skoda for about ten minutes and drove to a corner noodle spot. The shoulder of the road was packed with scooters, mopeds, bikes, and people were streaming in and out of the spot. All around us were construction sites, and I figured most people eating there were working nearby. The building probably wasn't ever intended to be a restaurant because the curb and the street were about three feet higher than the entrance, but they cut a moat between the street and the restaurant that now served as a sort of patio. Everyone sat on stools below street level with their torsos popping out above traffic, which made for a periscope-like dining experience.

"Eddie, this is Lu Zhou Lao Mian Gwan.* Very local place we come to eat noodles and have big sweat."

Sichuan being a hot place, you want to sweat while you eat to cool down. It's good for your circulation and inner chi. You'll see people eating soup, chilis, and hot food year round just to sweat.

"Do they serve dan-dan noodles here?"

"Ha ha, you got to be kidding me, man. I thought you are chef! Who still eat dan-dan noodles?"

"What do you mean? Dan-dan noodles is the most famous noodles from Sichuan! I wanted to try dan-dan noodles in Sichuan because I've never had a good bowl of Sichuan dan-dan noodles anywhere else."

"Man, you never have a good bowl because dan-dan noodles is not that good. It's old stuff. People think it is fun because vendors used to walk through the streets with stick on shoulder going 'dan-dan' with buckets on the end. Dan-dan is old shit for the tourists, nothing special."

"You don't like it because it's too basic?"

"It's small. *Dan-dan mian* too small."

"So you don't like it, but it's too small? You're a walking Woody Allen joke."

"Woody what?"

---

* Lu Zhou Old Noodle Shop.

"Never mind."

I never liked Sichuan *dan-dan mian*. First, because everyone got it confused with Taiwanese *dan-dan mian* that my dad grew up eating on Yong Kang Jie, which was a bone-stock-based noodle soup with crushed peanuts and *tza tsai*, spicy pickled radish. A classic and irresistible dish. As opposed to Sichuan *dan-dan mian*, which was just noodles sitting in chili oil with a half teaspoon of ground pork, sesame paste, and cilantro.

They were basically sesame butter and chili oil sandwiches, but everyone in America held this up as one of the canonical Sichuan dishes alongside *ma po tofu*, water braised chili beef (*shui ju niu*), and the equally unimpressive Sichuan beef noodle soup. I kept trying *dan-dan mian* in Chengdu just to make sure it wasn't terrible, because everyone who had visited Chengdu, from aunts and uncles to Fuchsia Dunlop, still swore by it. Yet, I still couldn't understand why Rabbi despised it.

"*Dan-dan mian* is famous, but locals don't eat it, Eddie. *Shu jiao zha jian mian** is better. You wouldn't go out for *dan-dan mian* because it's too small."

"OK, but what if someone sold it in a stall or food court as a snack, you still don't like it?"

"Naw, if I'm at the food court I'll get *liang mian* because it's bigger."

"FINE, so if it's the same size as *liang mian*, you wouldn't eat it?"

"EDDIE! I tell you, I can't explain why I don't like *dan-dan mian*, but it sucks. It is old shit like hot dog in America. People all know hamburger, but who wants shitty hamburger?"

"But I would show you a really good hamburger. I could take you to Peter Luger's or make one for you myself."

"So, *dan-dan mian* not like hamburger then because there is nowhere I can take you for great *dan-dan mian*. *Dan-dan mian* just not cool, man. I guess more like hot dog!"

"OK, hot dogs fucking suck, but I had a good one at Three Rivers

---

* Fresh pepper paste noodles.

Stadium in Pittsburgh. What about chili wontons? That's the same preparation as *dan-dan mian*, you like that, right?"

"What do you mean preparation?"

"You know, when you make *hao yo hwin dwin*."

"Oh yes, I see what you mean, yes, I like that, too. Wonton has more flavor and goes well, but noodle by itself, *dan-dan*, come on, man, you know better!" Rabbi said, exasperated.

"I actually don't, but you should show me."

"OK, we ask this guy, see what he think."

Rabbi turned to the table behind us eating a bowl of noodles. "Eh, *da gu*, my friend here is from America and he wants to try *dan-dan mian*, do you think there is a place you would recommend for *dan-dan mian*?"

With a head full of sweat and a bowl in his hand, son shook his head and chopsticks at us while the noodles waved from side to side out of his mouth.

"AHHH! *Dan-dan mian*? Who eats *dan-dan mian* still?"

"See, Eddie! *Dan-dan mian* like how you fools eat egg foo young! Ha ha, old shit, man."

After he marinated in his victory for a minute, Rabbi broke down the menu for me.

"OK, so here there is two styles: *gan mian* or *tang mian*. Dry beef noodles or chicken noodles with some stock. It's *lu zhou sin jiao niu roh mian* or *la ji gan dan mian*, so you pick."

"I want to try both."

"OK, we get both and share. Two bowls is too much for one person, even Human Panda like you."

We sat down at a folding table and grabbed the first two available stools as I watched them prepare the noodles. The reputation of hole-in-the-wall Chinese restaurants is that they're dirty and grimy, organized chaos, but Lu Zhou Lao Mian Gwan wasn't like that. Sure, having customers dine al fresco on a six-lane highway might seem bugged out, but in the eye of the storm, the kitchen was on point. Everything was organized assembly line–style with the cashier facing the street, away from a noodle station with one cook working two pots of boiling water. He pulled basket after basket of hot noodles out of the water and into bowls that were passed to him already filled with their proprietary noodle sauce, aromatic chilis, and garlic.

Every time the cook manning the noodle station pulled noodles out, homie with the bowls hit him in the breadbasket. It was like watching Peyton Manning run stretch right with Edgerrin James flanking him toward paydirt with garlic and chili confetti falling from the roof. On top of the noodles, they dropped a scoop of sautéed pork, chicken, or beef, depending on your order, and a grip of the requisite cilantro. But the meat wasn't just some Manwich mystery meat out of a can that your favorite lunch lady plopped on an enriched wheat bun. Every one of their meats was sautéed and seasoned with a different mixture. The pork got blessed with shallots, the beef touched by chili oil, and the chicken got a gang of pork fat. Our bowl came with ground beef and fermented chili paste to finish.

I quickly took the bowl, tossed the noodles with my chopsticks, took a whiff, and went HAM.

Instantly, my forehead beaded sweat, and I felt like I had just jumped off a thirty-foot diving board into a pool of fresh chilis. The first thing that hit my palate wasn't heat but the ice-cold freshness of red chilis. Common smoky dried chilis are like a big peppery glass of Bordeaux, but the chili-infused noodle sauce gave me that same feeling I had opening a bottle of Alain Graillot La Guiraude, expecting fruit but getting fresh salinity and cooling acid. For the non–wine drinker, think sour diesel cannabis. That cooling, almost minty flavor from a fresh bowl of diesel that wipes your mind like Windex and gives a ninja wings.

Clearly, there was heat, and my stomach was already rumbling, but from the waist up, I was refreshed. Usually, a sauce with soy, chilis, and garlic would be straight booty bass, but this shit came out crispy with horns like spottie ottie dopalicious angel.

"See, THIS CDC food, Eddie."

"Damn, that ain't no *dan-dan mian*."

For my second bite, I added some Chinkiang vinegar to see how it changed the dish.

"You like better this way, Eddie?"

"Yeah, I do. It's fresh with just soy sauce, but I like the extra acid with vinegar. It brings out the sugar in the fermented chilis."

"I agree, you see! That's why no one bother with *dan-dan mian*. So old and boring."

I got it.

"There are many ways to . . . how you say, 'finesse' chilis, right?" said Rabbi.

"HANH, you been watching the show, huh?"

"Yeah, man, we knows *Fresh Off the Boat*.* It's on the Travel Channel."

"What do you mean?"

"Your show. It's on the Travel Channel here. I just saw again last night."

"Wait, they show *Fresh Off the Boat* on the Travel Channel in China?"

"May not be same as Travel Channel in America, but what we call Travel Channel, sometimes they show your Taiwan episode."

"But we never sold the show to China."

"Oh . . . I don't know. Maybe you should calls them because it's definitely on TV here."

"That's bootleg, man! I thought you supported the culture."

"Don't worry, I buy lunch," said Rabbi.

The next morning I got up early. That Lao Mian Gwan had me thinking. I'd been making my mom's beef noodle soup forever. It was the one dish I could never make my own. Everything about it was hers, and I was happy with that.

Sometimes I'd boiled peanuts in the stock to give it more body, other

---

* *Fresh Off the Boat,* the original show on Vice, is now called *Huang's World.*

times soybeans, and sometimes I even whipped a little sesame paste into the bottom of each bowl just to freak it out, but I always went back to her recipe, and I wanted to make it for my friends in Chengdu.

"Yo! Evan, let's get ready to make beef noodle soup."

"I'm up, I'm up." He waved at me from his bed.

"It's ten A.M., we still need to get groceries, and it's going to take three and a half hours to make the soup, so let's get going."

"People aren't coming to eat until nine, we'll be fine. Leave me alone."

"Dude, we've cooked one time since we've been out here. Get your ass up."

"Man, I've been sitting here working on the Baohaus 2011 tax return every morning, so stop bothering me."

"Raf gave you almost a month off from working shifts to work on taxes, what else do you have to do?"

"A lot. . . ."

"Both of you need to shut the fuck up 'cause I'm trying to sleep," said Emery from under his covers. "You never should have had Evan do the taxes, Eddie, but, Evan, you've been dragging your ass not asking for help, so at this point you need to just finish it. It's not that hard, you just don't want to do it."

"I'm going to Treat. Evan, when I get back you need to help me gather all the equipment to cook downstairs."

I went to Treat for groceries alone. Things were bad with Evan. I could tell it wasn't the work, though. He was sick of being the younger brother. He needed to be his own man, and even if I was right, I just couldn't tell him nothin' no more.

I started just grabbing items and throwing them in the cart, thinking about all the things I was going to say to Evan. If he wanted to leave, he should just be a grown-ass man and leave, pay for his own shit! Do his own thing, but he didn't. He used Baohaus to support himself but didn't always do the work and stayed crunchy all the time. How you gonna take the money, not give 100 percent, and screw your face at me all the time? Fuck outta here.

Within the hour, I was back at Hakka Homes boiling the first* off the oxtails, pig's feet, and tendons when Evan walked in.

"What do you need me to do?"

"Toast the chilis and peppercorns, slice the ginger, cut the scallions. I'll handle the rest."

"Got it."

"And chop the cilantro."

"Anything else?"

"Cut the tomatoes, too."

"Stop for a second and tell me exactly everything you need to do 'cause you're just going to start throwing shit at me to do if you don't think it through right now."

"Man, fuck you. I give you all the easy shit to do. I'm still the one cooking it all, so who cares if I forgot to tell you to cut the mustard green, too. You see the shit. You've done this dish before. Just cut the shit you know I'm going to need."

"Dude, I quit. I fucking quit!" Evan turned to storm out.

I almost threw the pot of boiling animal firsts at his ass.

"Gimme my money back for your plane ticket and fly your ass home yourself, then, you little bitch."

"Take my money! Take everything! You already fucking wasted three years of my life following you around taking notes and doing all the shit work you don't want to do."

"What do you think you would have been doing? You're the one that went to Blue Hill for a week and decided to stay at Baohaus! I told you to leave mad times if you wanted to! You walked in a partner, fool! It's not my fault you didn't get ahead of the business and set up the books. Now we have to go back and retrofit the whole thing."

"You're the boss! You should set the systems up!"

"Then why are you a fifty/fifty partner? I'm the chef, you're the opera-

---

* First is the blood and gray foam that comes up when you flash-boil meat before braising it.

tor, but you don't operate shit! If I took your fifty percent and went on Craigslist I'd find somebody TODAY that would take your job."

"So go do it, then!"

"You're family! I'm not giving any part of the business to anyone but family. This is OUR SHIT."

"I don't want it!"

Just as Evan walked out, Emery walked in.

"Cot damn it, what the fuck is wrong with you two?" Emery asked.

"Evan quit!"

"Evan, get your ass back here!"

"I quit!" Evan yelled as he walked away, down the hallway.

I looked around the apartment with the smell of beef first boiling away. Ginger on the floor, cilantro scattered across the counter, and chili seeds stinging the skin under my fingernails. I didn't want to think about Evan. I just cooked.

"Ed, you OK, man?"

"I'm fine."

"What happened?"

"He quit."

I toasted and tossed chilis in a wok.

"I know, but why'd you argue?"

"It doesn't matter. He wanted to fucking quit. Evan never wanted to do the taxes. He left the shit for over a year because he figured someone would deal with it, and now that I'm making him do it, he wants to quit. He just wants to work with me when it's easy, but as soon as it gets hard, he quits."

"I don't think that's it, Ed."

"What do you think it is, then, huh? Fuck him!"

"Look, Evan sometimes takes the easy way out. Yes, it's easier to come work with you instead of doing his own shit, but that's not why he works with you."

"Yeah! He works with me because he knows that when shit hits the fan, I'll pick it up! I always pick it up. What's he gonna do when I'm not around?"

"Sometimes it's you, but sometimes it's him, too, man. When you needed to get out of the kitchen and write the book, who ran the shop?"

"He ran it like shit! I had to go in and tweak the minced pork one day because they cut corners browning the skin. There was also a whole week where they were butchering the chicken thighs wrong, giving away an extra half an ounce on every order!"

"Ed . . . are you listening to yourself? *He ran the shop for you for six months* and you're complaining about one day and one week where someone else in the kitchen fucked up. You hold him to a higher standard than yourself sometimes. It's not fair. You'd never put your whole life into someone else's project like Evan has with yours, and you know it."

"This isn't just mine. This is our whole family's story!"

"Yes, this is our family's story, but *you* are telling it! I love the book. I love Baohaus, but would I tell it the same way? No. That doesn't mean you're wrong, but you can't tell it for me. This is *your* version of our family story."

I was embarrassed. When I wrote the book and started the restaurant, I always tried to represent my family in a way they'd be proud of. I thought of what Emery would say, I asked Evan what he thought, I tried to surprise my parents with how well I knew them. . . . I knew I had good intentions throughout, but I was crushed in that moment. I'd forgotten my own maxim: no one or no thing can speak for you, you have to speak for yourself.

"I gotta make this soup, man. I don't have time for this fucking shit. You guys don't like how I represent the family, then I won't talk about our family anymore."

Emery didn't say a word.

I started to slice the ginger and kept to myself. Emery almost never helped out in the kitchen. It wasn't his thing, but with Evan gone he filled in. He didn't exactly know the dish, but he picked up the pot, cleaned up the cilantro, and did his best to reorganize my ingredients.

"Thanks, Emery."

I thought about adding more chilis than usual to appease Rabbi's

Chengdu tastes, but remembered what Mr. Zheng said about staying true to yourself. Fuck it. My temper got the best of me and I let the chilis go.

"Hmmm, that's a lot of chilis, Ed."

"That's what they want! I'm not fighting people anymore. Fuck what I think, just give people what they want. Fucking Chengdu people want to just burn their mouths! Who cares about nuance or the anise or the fucking acid in the tomatoes? You know, I don't even have to come out here and bring Evan or bring you or understand how Chengdu people feel about Americans cooking their food or care how Mr. Fusco thinks about me. Fuck everyone."

"Eddie . . . Calm down, man. You're not making any sense right now, and you're standing in a closet with a stove toasting chilis. Get out of here for a second."

"No. I want to make this soup."

"All right, well, I'm going outside because I can't breathe in here, but take it easy. . . ."

My mom once told me you can't cook angry. That you'd taste it in the food and just like all her mumbo jumbo about family, I didn't believe it anymore. All these stupid fucking Chinese proverbs made no sense. First it was that you could taste somebody's hand in a dish. Then it was that you could taste the anger in a dish. None of it made any sense; I just kept cooking. I seared my ginger, garlic, tossed in the chilis and peppercorns, then started to braise the oxtail, pig's feet, and tendons. When I opened the soy sauce, I noticed that the local brand was a little flat. They didn't have the brands I used at the store, so I asked the clerk for his favorite and he pointed me to this saltier, flatter, one-note soy sauce. Regardless, I had to use it.

A few hours later, I took my first taste of the beef noodle soup, and it wasn't bad. It had fewer layers because the chilis took over the ginger slightly and the soy sauce wasn't bright enough. It was different, but not bad. I wanted to see what Rabbi would think.

"Hey! Ed, you ready to start setting up downstairs?" asked Emery.

"Yeah, we still have two hours, but let's get the station set up. Take the two burners and the big pot for noodles, then fill it up with water when you get down there. I have bottled water I left out in the corner."

"All right, sounds good."

"And then come back up for the sides like pickled mustard green, cilantro, scallions, chili oil."

"All right. . . ."

"And . . ."

I stopped myself. I'd already driven Evan to quitting, so I pulled back just before I was about to set Emery off. Before I packed everything up to go down, I mixed a little Chinkiang vinegar and fresh chili to dip the pig's feet in if people wanted to pull it out of the soup and enjoy it that way. Downstairs, Emery had it all going. Butane burners were set up, noodle water was boiling, and he had all my utensils. I don't think Emery had been that helpful since the '80s.

"I did good, huh, Ed?"

"Thanks, Emery, I appreciate it, dude."

"No problem, brudder, we'll have fun."

"Yeah, we will."

"Hey, I went back to my room for a second and Evan was there. He was wondering if he could come eat later. He definitely still wants to quit, but he feels bad. And I think it's fucked up if he has to go eat somewhere else by himself tonight, ya know?"

"He can come eat, just tell his fake ass not to come talk to me."

"All right," said Emery warily.

We stood there in silence for a good ten minutes just stirring water aimlessly, watching it boil, bringing the soup back up to temp, and tossing cilantro to pass time like they were rosary beads.

"Did you call Mr. Fusco yet about Dena?"

"No. Who cares what he thinks?"

"What do you mean, man?"

At that moment Rabbi rolled up. He was about thirty minutes early.

"Hey man! Wassup!"

"Ehhh, just hangin' out."

"I thought this beef noodle soup party, you guys look bummy."

Neither of us said anything for a moment, but then Emery spoke up.

"Rabbi, did Eddie tell you one of the big reasons why he's here in China?"

"Yeah, to learn Chengdu food and see what we thinks about you ABC, ha ha."

"He's also proposing to his girlfriend here."

"WHAT? Player down! This is cool, man! Why you decide this, Eddie?"

"I was just flying over Mongolia a few weeks ago, and it hit me. She's the one."

"Eddie, man. . . . I have to tells you. You talking about 'the one' and you standing in front of beef noodle soup, but you sound like shit, bro. What's wrong?"

"I got in an argument with Evan. He quit working with me today."

Rabbi laughed.

"Big deal! He quit helping you with beef noodle soup one day, that's why you have two brother. He be back tomorrow."

"I think he's gone for good this time, man."

"Still . . . he stop working with you is one thing. He is still your family. And you have girlfriend coming soon, that is your new family. Nothing actually lost here. Plus . . . you have BEEF NOODLE SOUP. I want to try a bowl. Come on, man!"

In an effort to please our customer, Emery dropped the noodles into the still-not-boiling water.

"Ahhh, did you drop the noodles?" I asked.

"Yeah! Rabbi said he wants a bowl."

"All right . . . I guess we can let it go. Water's been heating up for a while."

"I think this is as hot as it's gonna get, Ed, it's been heating for thirty minutes."

Our butane burner at Hakka Homes was stupid weak and meant for hot pot. Even with a really small pot of water for noodles, it had trouble getting to the right temp. After a couple minutes, I could tell it wasn't going to work.

"Emery, pull the noodles, it's not hot enough."

He pulled out the noodles looking like a wet wig all stuck together.

"Gross, man."

"Damn, Eddie, I hope you don't serve like this in America," said Rabbi.

"Gimme a second, Rabbi, you're early! I gotta get this water to temp."

Emery dumped out the noodles and stared back at the water.

"Emery, we gotta take more water out of the pot. It's not going to boil with that much water."

"But the starch is going to build up if there's less water."

"I know, that's why you just gotta batch cook. I'll give you a little oil to toss the noodles, but we have to get ahead and batch cook, then reboil water."

"OK."

Nothing seemed to be working. Something as simple as boiling noodles became complicated because we could only boil three orders of noodles at a time before having to reboil the water.

"Ed, you should call Evan. We're going to need help setting the tables and taking the money if I'm doing the noodles like this."

He was right. We did need Evan, but I didn't care.

"Don't worry about it, I'll do the noodles, you just set the tables and take money. I can do noodles and soup."

About twenty minutes later, our first good bowl of noodles came out.

"Finally. . . . Here you go, Rabbi."

I dropped one piece each of oxtail, pig's foot, and tendon in his bowl with a slice of braised tomato and spinach as well.

"WOW! This is *real* Taiwanese beef noodle soup. We don't see this much."

Crawfish Zheng showed up.

"Hey! Xiao Ming, you already serving?"

"Yeah, eight P.M., just like you said!"

"Ha ha, all right, not bad. I can start my shift with a bowl of soup. I usually just get here at eight P.M."

Zheng's wife rolled up with all his stuff on a cart.

"Damn, you wheel everything here every night? I thought you'd have storage somewhere."

"Nope, every night, we wheel it in. Storage is expensive!"

"Wow, Eddie, this Taiwanese beef noodle soup is awesome! I like very much, just enough spicy, too. Last time I eat your red-cook pork, I like the bitter melon best because pork not spicy enough, but this time beef noodle very good."

"Man, Rabbi, you like anything spicy," I said, laughing.

"Yes, this Chengdu way! But this soup, I think Taiwan does better. I like how you use the anise and tomato. I think if you sell this in Chengdu very success. You would need to call Taiwanese beef noodle soup, though, and let people know. Even though spicy, flavor still much different than Chengdu beef soup."

Emery took a sip of the soup.

"Wow, that's spicy, man. It's good but spicy."

"You like it?"

"Yeah. Definitely different than Mom's, but I like it."

After giving Zheng a bowl, he chimed in as well.

"Hmmm, Xiao Ming, this is very good. Compared to the Taiwanese beef noodle soup I've had in Shanghai, it is spicy, but I see you did that for Rabbi. Besides the chili, it is balanced and after that initial sting, it really settles down and shows all the components. I like it very much!"

People started filing in one by one. Friends of ours, friends of Rabbi's, Hakka Heather, and even an English fan of the show who saw our photo on Instagram and came by with a handwritten piece of paper saying: "EDDIE LOVE BABY."

"EDDIE LOVE BABY!" screamed the English fan with his wife in tow.

"Do you know this guy?" asked Emery.

"Nah, but the love is mad real."

Rabbi and all the other Chinese people seemed bugged out by the exuberant Englishman, but he did have an Asian woman with him that seemed to temper the apprehension. At least one of us understood this man.

"EDDIE LOVE BABY, this is my wife! Lifelong Chengdu native, love of my life who saw on Instagram today you were here and we LITERALLY, I mean LITERALLY just left my brother's wedding to come see you. I said 'BABY, I got to see EDDIE LOVE BABY if it's the last thing I fucking do.' This is the realest man on the planet. He eats fucking PENIS LOVE POPSICLES in Taiwan, he rides the fucking BANG BUS, he defends the rights of slaughtered white rabbits, fuck, I love you EDDIE LOVE BABY, and I come bearing gifts. I have this tallboy for ya here, I got the sign, and we're buying noodles!"

"Dude, you left your BROTHER'S wedding to come eat beef noodle soup?"

"It was the reception, man, the real shit was already over, plus, IT'S YOU! IT'S EDDIE LOVE BABY!"

As this Englishman whose name I can't remember kept pouring out his love for me, from the right corner of my eye, I saw Evan walk over with his head halfway down, trying not to make waves with his arrival. Just then, the Englishman popped open a tallboy.

"EDDIE LOVE BABY! HERE'S TO YOU! CHEERS!"

And he proceeded to pour beer down his chin, his shirt, and the floor.

"Hai, baby, maybe you should let Eddie cook?" said his wife shyly.

"What are you talking about, it's not Eddie, it's EDDIE LOVE BABY! He's a fucking genius! He cooks with his eyes closed and his hands behind his back!"

"I actually don't, bruh. I can't even boil noodles today."

"Lemme back there! I'll give you a hand, EDDIE LOVE BABY!"

Emery was out talking to our friends, so the Englishman made a move toward the noodles. Just as he was about to park himself next to me, Evan cut in.

"Whoa, whoa, whoa, no worries, LOVE BABY! I got it, I got it. Take a seat, man, noodles are on us tonight."

"They are not! I'm a paying customer. I came to pay my respects to EDDIE LOVE BABY!"

"Dude, it's on us. I insist! Take a seat, drink the beer, noodles on us, I insist. You left your brother's wedding for this. You're gonna regret it the rest of your life."

"What are you talking about? This is the best day of my life! I even brought my book for you to sign, EDDIE LOVE BABY!"

Englishman finally took a seat, and Evan manned the noodles.

"You batch cooking these?" he asked.

"Yeah, man."

"Cool, I got it."

I always said, if I wanted to talk about socioeconomics and existentialism, I'd call Emery. But if I was playing sports or double dating, I'd call Evan.

Add cooking to Evan's column. All these years, I took it for granted that there wasn't another person in the world who could step in and cook right next to me like Evan, not even my mom.

"Can I try the soup, Ed?" asked Evan.

"Yeah, here's a spoon."

Evan took the wooden spoon, dug from the middle of the pot, drained some oil off and took a sip.

"Eh?"

He made a Jeff Van Gundy face. That not completely satisfied, not completely appalled, but absolutely completely torn about how to respond.

"It's different. It's not your normal beef noodle soup."

Even more than my mom's, Evan knew *my* soup. In a lot of ways, he grew up on my beef noodle soup. I didn't tell him what I did, holding out hope that maybe he would like it better than the soup he was used to.

"Just tell me what you did, numbnuts. It's not as good!"

"Fine! I put more chilis in 'cause you quit and I got mad! And this Chengdu soy sauce fucking sucks. Try it!"

I had all my ingredients with me under the table and gave Evan the soy sauce to try.

"Eck. It's that cheap, flat, salty soy sauce. I don't even know what people use that shit soy sauce for."

"I know, man, this soup sucks. . . . Rabbi likes it, though."

"Who cares if Rabbi likes it, he doesn't know what Taiwanese beef noodle soup is supposed to be like. He's a white person! If you put hot sauce on it, he likes it. Whiteness is EVERYWHERE!" Evan said, laughing.

"Ha ha, naw, Rabbi really knows Chengdu food, but you're right. That motherfucker loves hot sauce."

I needed Evan. He remembered my soup, even when I'd lost it. You meet new people like Rabbi or Mr. Zheng and they mean well. They give you their honest feedback telling you it's pretty good, like someone saying Michael Jordan was pretty good if they only saw him play for the Wizards. But Evan was the one person that could come out of the stands screaming, "I saw this motherfucker drop six threes on the Blazers in the '92 Finals and shrug it off 'cause he wasn't even a three-point shooter!"

"You're missing the brightness, man, and the acid. The tomatoes are muted because the chili overpowers them, and the soy sauce blows."

I got to work.

"Hey! Eddie, this is my friend, Tim! Taiwanese b-boy, he is here to try the soup," said Rabbi.

"Sorry, Tim! It's nice to meet you, but gimme a few minutes. Maybe have some of Zheng's crawfish first? I gotta tweak this soup."

"Oh, OK, no problem," said Tim, confused.

"What happened? That soup was good, man!" said Rabbi.

"No, it wasn't, it'll be even better," said Evan. "Just watch."

I started a new pot of aromatics. Garlic, scallions, dry chilis, peppercorns, and—this time—fresh chilis. It was something I'd never done before but figured out on the fly. Fresh chilis allowed me to add more bone stock, maintain the spice level for Rabbi, but also bring some fresh acid and brightness to the dish. To counteract the dull soy sauce, I snuck in a nugget of rock candy and increased the amount of ginger. Meanwhile, I boiled some fresh tomatoes in the beef stock to fortify that. After simmering for a good twenty-five minutes, it was all ready.

"OK! Taste it now."

Evan took his spoon, ladled it carefully, and took a sip.

"Damn. . . ."

"What? 'Damn' good or 'damn' bad?"

"Damn. . . ."

"Evan, what do you mean?"

"Son. . . ."

"Don't hold out on me!" I screamed with a wooden spoon in my hand.

"That's so good. Even better than before. It's like the first time Mom added tomatoes to the beef noodle soup and set it off. Combining the dry red chilis with the fresh chilis is genius. Now there are two types of heat and two types of acid plus the little bit of sugar carrying it all even further."

"I always thought you either use dried chilis or chili oil or chili paste or fresh chilis, but each one is different. I thought about *ma po tofu* and how Mom uses five different types of chili to create one chili flavor, and did it to the soup!"

"Man. Mom is gonna be so pissed," said Evan.

"Nah, Mom's gonna be proud," I responded.

I took another sip, gave Evan a slap on the back and thanked him for coming back.

"Rabbi! Soup's ready!" shouted Evan.

Rabbi walked over with Tim in tow, his old bowl still in his hands.

"Here, put in my old bowl is OK."

"You sure? Drink the rest of the soup so they don't mix."

Rabbi downed the last remaining bit of his soup and extended his hands. Evan dropped a basket of noodles, and I poured in the soup, topping it off once again with one each of oxtail, pig's foot, and tendon.

"Hmmm, this is cool. I don't usually see the pig foot or oxtail in Taiwanese beef noodle soup, very interesting move," said Tim.

After all this time, I'd almost forgotten that most Taiwanese people made the stock with beef bones and served it with sliced shank. I started doing it with oxtail, pig's feet, and tendon a few years earlier and never looked back, the flavor from the oxtail being superior to beef bones.

"Yeah, you get more viscosity with pig's feet and oxtail."

The two walked away, each with a bowl of soup, and sat down at the table. After a few minutes, I walked over to see what they thought.

"WOW!" said Tim ecstatically, with half a pig's foot in his mouth. "Eddie, this is how you say 'AWESOME,' eh?"

"Yes! I agree, Eddie. This soup is even better than thirty minutes ago. What did you do?" asked Rabbi.

"I mixed fresh chilis with dry chilis for two different types of heat. One smoky, one bright and acidic, so there's more layers."

"Tim, how does this compare to other Taiwanese beef noodle soup you had?" asked Rabbi.

"Rabbi, I have to say this is not Taiwanese beef noodle soup."

"Why's that?" asked Rabbi.

"This is just very unique. I don't know how to say besides this is original! I've never had like this. You can tell it comes from Taiwanese beef noodle soup, but many innovations."

Evan pulled me aside.

"Eddie, I think you should stop asking what everyone thinks, you and this soup are your own thing. Even at Old Jesse, you pissed me off, man. You don't have to keep bowing to everyone. Stop asking for approval. It makes me sad."

I wasn't sure what to say, but I was glad Evan had come back. I felt stronger when he was around. I guess my mother was right about the third chopstick.

"Sorry I quit like I did."

"It's cool. You can come back if you want."

"I thought about it a lot, Ed. I don't respect myself working for you. I don't know who I am, and you can't teach me. I gotta go."

My mother's vision of three boys together forever was impossible. A family can't move as one. A family has to grow, extend, get cut off, and grow again like succulents. If you believe in family, you know it's built for this. One day, we'll all come home. And then we'll go away again.

Emery had been listening to the entire conversation. In a stroke of unprecedented self-control, he bit his tongue and resisted saying a word until the coast was clear.

"Dickhead, let Evan go. You got Dena."

PART 3

NEW BEGINNINGS

Tim

"Hey, Eddie! Emery tells me something very disturbing!" said Rabbi, still in a haze from the soup.

"What? Something wrong?"

"I hear Dena is coming tomorrow, but you still haven't called her father!"

It was a sore spot with me ever since the phone call at Noah's Ark. Why did I have to ask? Why did he have to approve? This was some caveman shit, to think he owned her. After his whole rant about *The Firm* and Tom Cruise and China as this fucking evil communist country, I didn't feel like I needed his approval about anything in my life. I didn't understand why telling someone I loved her and that I wanted to be with her the rest of my life required me to kowtow to someone too ignorant to understand that communism in China was like freedom in America. A mirage.

Even with my parents, wrong was wrong. If I held my parents to a reasonableness standard, why would I lower the bar for Mr. Fusco? Humans should be reasonable if for no other reason than the fact that we *can* be reasonable. To lean on your status as a parent to justify your baseless, boneheaded opinions and actions is as archaic and ass-backward as breathing out of your mouth.

"I don't need his approval. Even if he said no, I would propose anyway. Why ask if his opinion doesn't matter?"

"Eddie. This is very shameful. It is not about whether he says yes or no, this is about respect. That is her father. He raised her and in a way you are taking her."

"I'm not taking her!"

"Of course you are. This is natural, though. It is OK. Every parent knows this and expects this, for the most part they want this. Especially father of the bride, this is a huge accomplishment for him! He raised a daughter that somebody wants to marry and be partners with. In many ways, this is his greatest achievement as her father. You cannot take this away from him," said Rabbi emphatically.

"I agree, Ed. The right thing to do is ask. Don't let him drag you down. . . . You already know this is how Americans think about us," added Emery.

"Eddie, if you don't have respect, what do you have? You can't not do this," said Rabbi.

I couldn't get over it. A part of me wanted to stick it to Mr. Fusco. Americans like him called me "communist" before I ever knew what communist meant. I had nothing to do with communism and even if I did, so what? Communism is an ideology with good intentions that got applied to the world in extremely grotesque ways, just like religion or democracy or fertilizer!

At the most base level, I felt trapped. I found my wiz, but before I could walk with her into the rest of my life, I had to bow to a white man once again.

I packed up the leftovers and equipment, thanked Mr. Zheng, and brought it all upstairs to my apartment. Tim helped me with everything because Rabbi had to get to the club across the street and DJ. I grabbed my jade one-hitter from Mongolia and ran downstairs to hotbox Tim's car; I hadn't smoked for two weeks.

"Here, I don't know if it's good, but this is as good as it gets in China," offered Tim.

It wasn't good. It wasn't even close to good. It was vintage hot trash middle-school dance party weed that came with sticks, stems, and now Mongolian one-hitters. I took a puff.

"This tastes like shit, bruh," I said, laughing.

"Ha ha, take it easy, Eddie, this is what we deal with here."

"Would you rather have fast internet or better weed?" I asked.

"Oh . . . of course better weed, then you don't notice the internet."

"TRUE! Yo, what do you do out here?"

"You guess."

"What do you mean? You want me to guess your job?"

"Yes, what do you think? Look at me, guess my job."

"I mean, Rabbi told me you're a b-boy, so I figure that's your job."

"Yes, I b-boy and have a studio with my friends, but I am in dental school here."

"Ha ha, that's wassup, man. How am I supposed to guess you in dental school from how you look, though?"

"I'm just saying, I want you to guess so you remember that I don't look like a dental school student."

"Aight. I get it. I went to law school, but I don't look like a lawyer, I don't think."

"No, you are not. That is why you are an inspiration to many Taiwanese kids like me, Eddie."

It caught me off guard. After a month in China, I had forgotten about my American existence, especially the notoriety.

"Thanks, man, I appreciate it. I always wanted to know what Taiwanese people think about the things I say." My desire for acceptance crept up on me again.

"I will tell you!"

"Word?"

"Yes! I have followed your whole career from Chengdu and Taiwan. In the beginning, many newspapers in Taiwan wrote that you were a bad kid. You didn't listen to your parents. You quit law school and even though you were successful many people felt like you should still be a lawyer."

"That's funny! In America, everyone gets it and encouraged me to follow my dreams."

"I know! But you see, the first thing people think about you in Taiwan is that you disrespected your parents. They can't get over that. Even I thought it was crazy to go through law school and then ignore your parents' wishes, but then I went to dental school myself. It sucks, man! This isn't me. In Taiwan, I was a b-boy. I never wanted to be a dentist, but my parents told me to, so I listened. For many of us, we have no choice. How do you say no to parents that have given you everything they have?"

It was funny to have the conversation with Tim. In America, being a b-boy is an ethos, and while there are your weekend warriors who may or may not also work as dental hygienists, it's not that ill to say it out loud or think about in those terms. B-boy shit is just something you do. It's not at odds with the other things you're doing in your life, even if it may be funny to see the dude who just gave you a root canal do windmills under the Brooklyn Bridge on Saturday afternoon. It's an extension of your essence. Even as an attorney, I did the work, but it didn't change who I was. Connie served everything on two plates, and I once turned in a legal memorandum with beef noodle soup stains.* No matter how hard the Man tries to sterilize us, I take solace in the fact that we can't be erased.

"That's their choice, though, Tim. Just because your parents chose to have kids, doesn't mean you choose to have them run your life. That's not the point of having kids."

"Now I agree. I am going to finish dental school for them and show them I can do it, but I want to go to America."

"Word? Why not just stay in China? Your parents are in Taiwan. They aren't going to come get you."

"I know. But in China, I am considered Taiwanese. I don't necessarily fit in here, either. I am used to Taiwan and just the way we are restricted around the city . . . it's different. It gets depressing here. I just can't go back because my parents will control me there."

---

* I had written this legal memo, printed it out, then eaten a bowl of beef noodle soup by the computer. Since it was a first draft, I didn't think it was a big deal to save paper and turn it in as-is . . . but it was a big deal. I ended up having conversations with multiple people about "decorum." Considering that Japanese businessmen presented business cards with two hands and a bow, they were probably flabbergasted at how the child of Japanese occupation thought it was OK to turn in memorandums with beef noodle soup. #GreenThumb

"You think you aren't going to be different in America?"

"I don't know how to explain, Eddie. America just seems more free. Life is hard in China. I want to go somewhere no one expects anything from me."

"That's just the beginning. I understand that you want a new beginning. That's how a lot of overseas Chinese feel; our lives began interrupted. But that's all it is, a beginning."

I couldn't quite wrap my head around what I was trying to say, so I took another hit as Tim waited. I didn't want to let him down. I could tell that he knew more about me than I did about him, and he was expecting something. He'd been anticipating this conversation and we'd connected, but I had to figure out how to say it.

"So you really not going to ask her dad for permission, huh?"

"I don't know, but I still want to figure out what I'm trying to tell you."

"Yes, please!"

"What I'm trying to say is, don't put so much pressure on yourself or China or America. They're all doors. You walk through one door, you open another door, you may like this room or that room and the next one, but it's never the end or actually the beginning. Orlando taught me to appreciate New York. I wouldn't understand it if I hadn't spent twelve years wandering gas stations and cul de sacs. New York is my home but Orlando was my motivation."*

"Eddie, man, I feel like what you say is very powerful, but I don't think I understand."

"It's cool, man. I don't think I understand, either. I just had to try."

I took another hit and reclined the seat.

"This weed ain't so bad," I said, laughing.

After we smoked the last of Tim's weed, we headed across the street to Jellyfish where Rabbi was DJ'ing. It was in a huge strip mall upstairs with kids hanging out all around the complex. There were stands selling

---

* As I said it, I could hear Young in my head goin' "That's riiiight!"

skewers, pastries, drinks, cigarettes, and newspapers all around. Everyone was Chinese downstairs, but once you got upstairs it was full of international people, i.e., white people and the upwardly mobile colors of Benetton. The bouncer kept stopping Chinese people at the door but let all the international people in.

"Yo, why can't the Chinese people get in?" I asked Tim.

"They don't have money. Unless it's really good-looking girl or guy with money, they don't get in."

"Then why they letting in these wack-looking white people?"

"If you are white in China, you probably have money. Plus, white is 'cool,' man. If a club has white people, everybody wants to come. Means it is hip. If good enough for white people is definitely good enough for Chinese."

"That's so fucked up."

"In America, though, isn't it cool to have black people in club?"

"Ha ha, you right. Black people do bring credibility to a party, but the clubs only want a few without Timberlands, fitted hats, and jerseys. Once there are too many black people, everyone goes to new clubs."

"That sucks, man."

"The world sucks, Tim. It's not just China."

We got into the club and found Rabbi upstairs. I looked up from the dance floor as he played Katy Perry and caught his eye. He put his hands on his headphones and shook his head in embarrassment. We walked over to him.

"Rabbi! Why are you playing this shit, man?"

"The owner make me! He crazy Israeli, but he know what international wants. They don't want that real shit, man." He had to shout over the noise and pointed over to a table.

"I have a table, though, you should go hang."

Tim and I walked over to his table, but they had buckets of beer and the requisite glasses for small children. You saw these glasses everywhere. They were the same tumblers I used to use for brushing my teeth as a kid, now repurposed for bottled beer service in a Chinese club.

"Tim, do they have liquor here?"

"Yes, they do. Johnnie Walker, Grey Goose, all that stuff, but if you get it, you will end up drink by yourself."

"Why?"

"We all just here to support Rabbi. Nobody want to get too fucked up 'cause this party not that fun."

"If none of you guys like it, why does Rabbi DJ here?"

"Because, Eddie, I try to explain this to you. This is hottest party in town. People that are into international-style party with big clubs come here. But normal Chengdu locals don't really come here because they can't get in. If locals go out, they probably go to Jiu Yan Qiao."

"Well, where do you go?"

"I come here," Tim said.

"But you don't like it?"

"OK, I explain. I come here because it's supposed to be 'cool' and you can meet girls, but I don't think it's actually fun. And Rabbi gets paid."

I understood what Tim was saying. The weed definitely had us stuck, but this was like Meatpacking District mega-clubbing. It was corny, it wasn't fun, but it was expensive and if your friend got a table for free you should probably take advantage and try to pick up girls. It always turned out terrible, but you went just to make sure it was still as terrible as you remembered it.

We sat there for a good fifteen minutes watching Rabbi play Katy Perry, Pitbull, and Flo Rida, before I called 'nuff.

"Tim, we gotta get outta here. Let's go to Jiu Yan Qiao."

"OK, but Jiu Yan Qiao can be dangerous."

"DOPE."

We got back in the car and drove about fifteen minutes to Jiu Yan Qiao. Along the way, Tim told me two stories.

The first was from a couple years ago when Tim went to the club pretending to be a tourist so that girls thought he had money. Anyone in China who has money to travel is probably well off. With his Taiwanese accent, it wasn't hard for Tim, so he took the girl back to a hotel and smashed, but the entire time she kept offering him chewing gum. Before they smashed, after they smashed, and figuring she was giving him a hint about his breath, Tim took it. . . .

Thirty minutes later, everything started melting, his vision got blurry, and Tim knocked out. When he woke up the next morning, he looked around the room and his wallet was gone. Then he told me a story of the time he fought Tibetan gangsters in the club and had a bottle cracked over his head. When I asked him what happened to the Tibetans, he said they got deported. Tibetans don't go to jail in China, they just get sent back, never to party in China again.

Once we parked the car, we walked toward the street that was pop-pington, but not in a Meatpacking or Jellyfish mega-club kind of way. The neon lights flickered, there were bottles on the ground, and street walkers all around. I'd call it grounded. This was the part of town desig-nated for selling seedy nightlife to Chengdu locals. It didn't need all the amenities of Shanghai or Jellyfish because people knew what time it was. I actually felt more at home; it was basically Chengdu's Chinatown.

"Where do you like going here?"

"I dunno. I kind of just walk the street. The clubs are expensive, and the bars are too dirty."

"Let's check it out, though."

It felt like Rabbi and Tim had been hiding this part of town from me, ashamed of how it would affect my perception of Chengdu. I realized I'd been "managed."

I walked into a club that looked like Mansion, but immediately some-one followed me in.

"Hey, do you know someone here? What is your name?"

"Xiao Ming, I don't know anyone here," I said in Chinese.

Immediately, they could tell I was Taiwanese from my accent and said as much. Tim came in behind me and assured the bouncer that I was Taiwanese and indeed had money to spend. Within minutes, we were swarmed by waiters looking to sell tables and girls that wanted to get booked. They grabbed my arms, rubbed their thighs against my legs, and caressed the small of my back. If you were ever curious what it felt like to be a girl in the club or a ribeye in a shark tank, go to Jiu Yan Qiao.

Looking to avoid getting robbed, we left the club after I took a piss.

"Damn. . . . They're aggressive in there."

"You wanted to come here! Locals very aggressive about getting your money. That's why international don't come here."

"These hos got the persistence of HPV."

"These hos got something," said Tim, laughing.

We walked around the block and saw the same scene outside the same clubs, but eventually reached a stretch of bars with live singing.

"You like these spots?"

"Not really, but we can check out. It's local people's karaoke singing. Have you done the high-class karaoke, though?"

"Yeah, I fucking love karaoke."

"What do you sing?"

"'Careless Whisper,' 'End of the Road,' 'Hey Ma,' 'Iron Lion Zion,' 'Bump n' Grind,' just the hits."

Luckily, the bar had dice. We got a few beers, played some dice, and listened to locals sing Chinese pop songs.

"You really like playing the dice, huh?"

"Yeah, I did it in Beijing and miss it. No one has this game in America."

"This is old stuff. So weird that you like it!"

"It's different, man. You're just used to it."

I sat at the bar for a good hour listening to people sing terrible Chinese pop records with the smells of dead fish and rotten vegetation drifting off the polluted river behind me, eating peanuts fried in recycled oil. After a few minutes, a raggedy-ass homeless dude covered in dirt, shirt and shorts ripped, with no shoes came over to me with a monkey on a leash. The monkey was visibly trying to run away from its owner, screaming and kicking as it got yanked by the collar. All around Chengdu and Shanghai, I'd seen the same hustle. Guys like this would wait outside karaoke joints, high-end restaurants, and clubs where women would come out around 2 or 3 A.M. stumbling, wanting a photo with the monkey. Unfazed by homelessness, I ignored the monkey and looked away.

But the monkey grabbed my leg. I tried to shake it off, but the monkey kept coming, and its owner barked at me in a heavy Sichuan accent to take a photo.

"I don't want a fucking photo!"

"Take the photo! Take it! Monkey want you to take it!"

But it didn't. The monkey didn't want me to take a photo. It was trying to run away from its owner. Every time he pulled the leash to bring the monkey closer, it hissed at him, kicked at him, and spat at the floor like Homeless Nate's* shawty on Orchard Street. But this wasn't a domestic dispute.

It was a different kind of slavery. I looked at the monkey: eyes jumping out of its head, tearing at its collar, screaming to get away with its face bright red, patches of hair missing as well. I still remember the way it hissed and screamed to get free like a mini-human with fur. It didn't look like an animal in the sense that there was separation between us. It was fam, and I tried to understand how someone could do this to family.

This was the humanity that was slowly coming into focus for me: something raw and exposed, something primal, something rotten that the matrix in this region hasn't corrected yet. Living in a civilization with the latest software updates, we forget that human nature is the same in America; it's just autocorrected and cleansed of Chingrish. Watching the homeless man yank the monkey chain, I saw the dark shadow humanity casts over all life.

I looked at the monkey again, and it appeared to be suffocating. It kept running toward me with its eyes wide and watering, grabbing at the collar around its neck. The homeless man had nearly choked the life out of the monkey, leaving just enough for photos.

I stared at that monkey waiting for it to tell me something.

----

* This homeless guy Nate and his boo were always fighting outside of Bereket on Orchard Street.

People talk about escape, but I don't believe in traveling for the purpose of forgetting. I travel to find myself again.

When I'm in an unfamiliar place, I gain negative space: the silence in confusion is all-knowing. Even hearing people speak a language or dialect you don't understand allows you to hear yourself. You can watch them mouth the words, speak with their hands, but everything's kind of in slow motion. A conjuring. You can see intention in the motions.

When you're transported and exposed to something different, you have to think. You gotta work. You gotta learn the Earth's vibrations all over again. You pay attention and you feel alive. You remember everything you forgot, and if you really really open your fucking eyes you may learn something new. Or find something old. Even in a world of enslaved monkeys and insidious chains, we can live with grace, respect . . . and tradition. It was time to call Dena's dad.

The phone rang twice, and my heart raced.

He picked up.

"Eddie! How's it going, pal?"

"I'm good, Mr. Fusco, how are you?"

"I'm great. Great. You know, we're doing great."

"Ha ha, that's great."

"Yeah, you know, I know Dena's going to China tomorrow!"

"I'll be there to pick her up. It might be the only thing I'm on time for this year."

"Oh, you better, Eddie, you better! That's my baby, you know."

"I know. . . . That's what I wanted to talk to you about, Mr. Fusco."

My hands started to shake a little bit. It felt the same way I used to feel when I was going to speak publicly or punch someone in the face. But I wasn't here to punch anyone in the face; I was here to respect. But what if I respected wrong? How the fuck do you do this? How do you ask someone for permission to marry his daughter? I really hadn't thought this through.

"What's up, Eddie? Tell me."

"Look, I don't want to dance around this. I just gotta tell you. I love Dena. I have never felt this way about somebody and it's not a fleeting, juvenile, like, 'oh, I just have a crush on her' thing. I love her. I love everything about her. She's a good person, she makes me happy, and she's my partner. I want to take care of her the rest of her life and be with her."

"Wow, Eddie, my heart's racing a million miles an hour right now. Geez Louise. Wow. I don't know what to say. As a father, you know this day is coming sometime, but you just never expect it. Holy cow!"

"I know. We're different, you and I, but I feel the same way, Mr. Fusco. It's crazy. I am asking for your blessing because I'm flying Dena out to China . . ."

I had to take a breath.

"Because I want to propose to her."

"Eddie," Mr. Fusco said and paused. "Eddie, you got it, buddy. You got it."

"Thank you, Mr. Fusco. Thank you. You know, I thought for a while about not calling. I was going to propose regardless of what you said because I love her. It's not about the institution of marriage, it's more the statement of love. So I thought about calling Mrs. Fusco to see what she thought, but I figured I should just call you. In both our cultures, for all the rights and wrongs and differences, we both know in this situation, I'm supposed to call you."

"You're right, Eddie. It's the right thing to do. And I gotta tell you, I respect you for it. I do. You did the right thing, buddy."

I'm not sure it was right. It kind of just was. I wanted to cross a bridge so I paid the toll.

I paid the toll, I asked the father, and I felt like a monkey.

Fish

"Eddie, you go down the stairs there, underneaths to the terminal, then look for sign to arriving and you find her. We wait here in Skoda mobile, man," said Rabbi, standing outside the airport.

"OK, thanks, Rabbi. I'll be back in a second."

"No worries, Eddie, *man zhou*,"* said Fish.†

The day had come. Dena was arriving.

I'd been planning for weeks with Rabbi and Fish. After paying respects to Mr. Fusco, I wanted to pay respect to the gods. Not in an organized religious way, but in a personal, spiritual, and cultural way.

Since the gods led me to Dena, it was time to pay respects at Emei Shaan,‡ one of the four sacred Buddhist mountains of China in Leshan. According to legend, Emei Shan belongs to Buddha's oldest son,§ Puxian, who also happens to ride white elephants with six tusks on a lotus leaf instead of holding a bus pass. King Jaffe Joffer and Kanye could have a son named Far East Akeem Kardashian West, and he STILL ain't seen excess until he seen crosstown, six-tusked, WHITE elephant cab Buddhist excess.

---

*   Walk slow. It's an expression people say like "good luck" or "take care."

†   You may have wondered where Fish had been all summer, after the red-cooked pork dinner. He lived primarily in Leshan and had to give tours of Tibet.

‡   Emei Mountain.

§   After doing research, some people say that he is not Buddha's son, but people in town and local legend told us that he was. Regardless . . .

I wanted Dena to see CHINA like I'd seen it and known it and, even in Orlando, lived it. I was all she knew about China. To her, I was the single manifestation of a five-thousand-year-old culture. It was time for her to meet the parents.

I couldn't wait to see Dena.

Before we picked her up, I'd been rolling around Chengdu with Rabbi trying to find a place that could fade my hair or even had clippers for sale so that I could blend my own damn hair. It took hours, but we finally settled on a salon for broke men that felt like a karaoke gigolo bar did a hostile takeover of the Hair Cuttery. Every stylist had a haircut like Justin Bieber, threaded eyebrows, and black button-down shirts unbuttoned to the pecs. I ended up teaching these goons how to fade, shape up, blend, and pull ice pick sideburns like I was instructions on the back of chopsticks. With my John Starks No. 3 Knicks Nylon Away Jersey and skin to 1.25 fade, I was ready to burn my player pass.

"Dena!"

I saw her wheeling her bag down the hallway with sneakers and a pink dress on. For a second, it felt weird. I hadn't seen her in so long, she felt distant. Her smile was excitement with a dash of hesitation and possibility of rain. I smiled awkwardly.

What the fuck, b? Why are you thinking about this? It ain't a first date! Just be yourself, I thought.

I couldn't help it, though. I went to kiss her and I could tell that it came off mad stiff, like pressing a toothbrush to her lips.

"Hey!" she said, pulling back and laughing.

She ran her hands over my fade.

"You look cute when you get your hair cut."

"Thanks, boo."

"Do people do fades out here?"

"They do now."

"Ha ha, it looks good."

"Ehhh, it's aight. White girls won't notice."

She pinched my arm. "Ohhhh, you're the woist!" she said.

"Ain't shit changed out here," I joked.

It was back.

"You hungry?" I asked.

Pops always told me, the first question you ask anyone when you pick them up is *"Tse lu fan ma?"**

"Yeah! Let's eat."

I took her bag and walked her out hand in hand.

Outside, Rabbi was eagerly awaiting us right at the foot of the stairs. Son was so close that he literally had to back up so that we could walk out.

"Dena! This is Dena! I have been watching you fly!" screamed Rabbi.

Rabbi's sister Mei Mei was also with us that day. She was so excited; she kept telling me how hard it was to pretend that she didn't know I was proposing. When Dena came down the stairs, I saw Mei Mei jump and clap her hands, then immediately stop herself.

It made me laugh.

"Watching me fly? What do you mean?" asked Dena.

"I mean, shit, uhhh, you know, I watch you fly. I check the flight, watch you fly," Rabbi said as his English began to fail him in his excitement.

"Ohhh, you've been watching the flight. I get it."

"Yes, yes, I watch it," he said, deadpan.

"Dena, this is Rabbi. Pronounce 'Ra-bee,' not 'Ra-bye.'"

"This guy always want to rub it in. So I teaches the Torah, big deal."

"Wait, Rabbi is Jewish?"

"Nooooo. It's like this. I thought Rabbi sounded cool, so I pick as my English name and everyone call me Rabbi, then one day I find out what a rabbi really is. I do not am Jewish, so then I say my name is 'Ra-bee not Ra-bye,' but you still spells like Rabbi."

"Rabbi, I give you a hard time, but did you know in the NFL there is a guy named Priest Holmes? If you ever make it to the NFL, it won't be weird at all that you are a Chinese running back named Rabbi."

---

* Have you eaten?

"I think you fucking with me, right? This is that thing you told me. . . . Irony!"

"Eddie, is this what you've been doing all month, just giving poor Rabbi a hard time teaching him about irony?"

"Yes! Yes! This what Eddie do, Dena. We show him all of Chengdu best food, most fun, then he make fun of us and teach us the irony. He really is like-a the Seinfeld."

"Anyway, I'm Dena!" she said, turning toward Mei Mei. I don't think she fully understood what I was saying about football or irony in China, but Dena had a way of absorbing confusing information on a surface level and then wiping the slate clean of awkwardness with her charm.

"Hi . . . hi," said Mei Mei quietly. She couldn't speak English.

"She is very pretty, Eddie!" Mei Mei whispered to me in Chinese, then covered her mouth to laugh.

"She says you really pretty, Dena."

"Ohhh, thank you, Mei Mei." She gave a blush and a smile, then tapped Mei Mei's shoulder in gratitude. I'd never seen this pageant queen version of Dena. It was intriguing to see her with three Chinese people in the palm of her hand like she was Miss America, but I had to blow her cover.

"Don't get gassed, she's never seen white people so she probably thinks you Julia Roberts," I poked.

"You are the worst!"

"Yes, yes, I agrees, Dena. Eddie definitely the worst," said Rabbi.

"This is Fish!" I said.

"Hi, Fish, I'm Dena."

"Hello! Fish," said Fish, pointing to himself.

"Yes, Fish," Dena reiterated.

"Yes, Fish," he said again as I realized the poor guy had just about run out of English phrases. Fish gathered his thoughts and then spoke again.

"I . . . I hear, uhhh, many things . . . ABOUT YOU! Yes, I hear many good things about you." There was extra emphasis as he struggled for each word, but I was proud of him. Fish was speaking some dope English.

"Thank you, Fish!"

Fish immediately went to grab Dena's bags, and I fought him for them.

"Xiao Ming, please, let me, you must," said Fish, and I relented.

We all packed into the Skoda and took off.

"Dena . . . ahhh, do you like-a the spicy?" asked Rabbi as he got right down to business.

"Yeah! I like spicy. Eddie gives me a hard time, though. He says white people just put hot sauce on things when they don't get it."

"It's true! Hot sauce speaks so well," I blurted.

"Hmmm, Eddie say many things about America and white people, but I will ask you myself because I do not trust Eddie's information. He too irony," said Rabbi.

"Ha ha, yes, any questions about white people please direct them my way, Rabbi."

"OK, so you like the spicy," he confirmed.

"Yes."

"Then we take you for your first Chengdu meal for hot pot! This is very famous in Chengdu. You must try."

Not fully understanding what was going on, Fish and Mei Mei forwarded all their mid-conversation questions to Rabbi and would ask him to translate what was said every thirty seconds. We continued the rest of the night speaking for thirty seconds, waiting for Rabbi to translate, fielding questions from Fish and Mei Mei, then proceeding to speak again.

It wasn't a burden, though; it was the best basketball game I'd ever been a part of. To watch Mandarin, English, Scranton, Chengdu, and New York run the motion offense in a Skoda mobile was my mountaintop. There was constant movement, everyone was unselfish, and you never knew where the next joke was coming from.

I think the satisfaction was all over my face, too. Dena kept squeezing my hand when I smiled.

"You look different!" she said.

"Oh yeah?"

"Did you lose weight?"

"I hope so! I been ballin' out here and eating less processed food."

"I can tell. You just look different."

"I'm happy," I countered.

We pulled up to Da Zhai Men Hot Pot right across from Hakka Homes. There were always waits of thirty minutes to an hour at Da Zhai Men. We usually avoided the lines and just went to more in-the-cut local hot pot joints, but with Dena in tow we decided to do it big. Da Zhai Men is a brand name. You get a mega-restaurant with multiple rooms, picture menus, and all the pageantry of a Cheesecake Factory plus duck intestines and pig's blood. Sometimes, the universe lets you have it all.

"Eddie, should we order the *yuan yang guo*? The two flavors with one mild or all spicy for Dena?"

"She eats more spicy than me, dude, but get *yuan yang guo* for me. I like to switch it up."

"OK, is there anything she don't eat? Or too funky for her?"

"Nope. She gotta try it sometime."

"Do it big, Rabbi," said Dena fearlessly.

"OK. . . . I think if you gonna do it big we should have lamb, fresh fish balls, duck intestines, duck tongue. . . ."

Intuitively Mei Mei picked up on what was going on.

"Get the fried sticky rice dessert with black sugar syrup! It is famous here."

"Yes, yes, we does that, too."

Then Fish jumped in.

"We should order fish, too!"

"Why do we order fish?" asked Rabbi.

"Because I am here! Right?" Fish said, looking around to see if anyone understood his joke.

"Oh my God, DYING," said Dena, laughing.

"Ha ha, you a goon, Fish," I said.

"We are not ordering fish at hot pot!" said Rabbi.

Fish slumped for a second and played sad. He knew what time it was.

We rounded out the order with beef tripe, fatty beef wrapped around enoki mushrooms, pig's blood, river eel, and *wai jui bai jioh*.

"This is Eddie favorite *bai jioh*, Dena. Have you had this before?" asked Rabbi, holding up a bottle of *wai jui bai jioh*.

"No! I haven't ever had *bai jioh*."

"Really? We have the Moutai at home."

"No, it smells so crazy when you open it, so I never tried it."

"Well, here we go, *gan bei*!" said Rabbi.

Dena picked up her glass with trepidation but under the pressure of cultural exchange, she took it down. It was a thing with us. If I asked her to try something, she'd do it for me, but I wanted to see the culture stand on its own two feet in her eyes.

"OHHHHHHH, that burns good," said Dena.

"Let's do it again!" said Rabbi.

"Are you sure?" said Dena.

"One more, Dena, Rabbi's hosting," I said.

We took down one more.

"Ahhh, that was good. Ready to eat," said Rabbi, satisfied. I think he felt the same way. This wasn't just meeting my girl. For Rabbi and Fish and Mei Mei, this was meeting America. Just like I represented Taiwanese-Chinese culture in America with everything I did, it was Dena's turn.

I hear a lot of people talking about Chinese hot pot like it's Japanese shabu-shabu or Korean barbecue, assuming that it's all about the quality of meat. Of course, you're going to have better hot pot with better meat, but there's really a lot of skill to hot pot. Very few people make a good broth. The problem is that hot pot is pretty fucking good, even if you just boil meat in chicken soup and dip it in sesame paste with garlic and cilantro, so most heads aren't discerning. For me, good hot pot is all about the broth, and a good broth tastes like Chinese medicine.

If you've taken Chinese medicine soup, you're familiar with the homies Amomi Fructus Rotundus, the god Fructus Jujubae, Citri Reticulatae Pericarpium, or Glehniae Radix. Hot pot is probably the closest thing in strategy that Chinese cooking has to offer to, say, curry. It's a concatenation* of herbs and spices that create something totally brand new, even if they make no sense when looked at as parts. It's the dissonance and conflict and difference between the spices that makes great hot pot. Everything fits because it doesn't.

"Cot damn, this is good," said Dena.

"Yeah, better than the joint by the Fung Wah station, right?"

"So much better. I can't explain it. It's just so much louder and complex. It's not even the same. Totally different thing."

"You can't even get Sichuan peppercorns that smell this good in America. Their regular peppercorns smell fresh, like green peppercorns in America, and the green ones are just outta here."

"Here! Try the duck intestine, Dena. It is Chengdu specialty," said Rabbi earnestly. He did the same thing with me when we went out for hot pot. He was all about the duck intestine.

"Take like this, Dena," he said, holding up one strand in his chopsticks as he dropped them into the broth.

"And shake, shake the whole time, only like ten seconds, then pull out before overcooked and taste!"

Dena took her chopsticks, picked up the intestine, shook it in the broth, and waited. After a few seconds, she took it out, blew it cool, and took a bite.

"That's incredible. It's snappy, but not chewy, and it just picks up the flavor of the broth without any funkiness. It's super clean."

"Yes! Yes! This is it, you got it, Dena," said Rabbi.

Dena was off to the races. Everything Rabbi offered her, she absorbed. After the first hour, everyone eased up and there was less trepidation on both sides. It became less of a tit-for-tat cultural exchange and we just

---

* I learned this word after reading Joshua David Stein's article about *Fresh Off the Boat* and promised to use it in book two. So there you go, a proper use of concatenation. . . . Shouts to Joshua David.

played. Dena tried everything and then settled on her favorites, Rabbi kept drinking *bai jioh*, and I smiled. Who needs a home when you have the diaspora?

Other people are bright; I alone am dark.
Other people are sharper; I alone am dull.
Other people have a purpose; I alone don't know.
I drift like a wave on the ocean, I blow as aimless as the wind.
I am different from ordinary people.
I drink from the Great Mother's breasts. *

The next morning Dena and I woke up together and started packing for our trip to Emei Shan, but something was wrong. Every time I bent over to pick up a pair of socks or squatted to fold clothes into my duffel bag, there was a sharp pain in my back and a rumbling in my stomach.

"Oh boy, is that you?"

"Yeah, my stomach is on fire."

"Is it from last night?"

"It has to be. I didn't really eat anything but hot pot yesterday and there's a cool hot sensation like I ate a tube of BenGay."

"Did you poop already?"

"Yeah, I had to shower, it was so bad."

"When are you going to start wiping sitting down, dude?"

"I did it after you told me, but I felt like the human little teapot about to fall over. I like standing up."

"You're a psycho."

"Leave wiping sitting down to quadrupeds; bipeds should wipe standing up and then shower after."

We got all our stuff together and left Hakka Homes.

Before heading to the bus station, Dena needed to exchange her money, so we went to the bank on the corner. As soon as we walked in,

---

* Tao Te Ching.

there was a thirtysomething Chinese guy with a shaved head and a messenger bag barking us over.

"Hey! Hey, buddy! You trying to exchange money?"

We ignored him, figuring he was a hustler.

"Hey! Come on, man, I'm asking you a question. Are you exchanging money for this American girl?"

When we approached the exchange counter, the bank tellers were all giggling.

"Hi, we need to exchange money."

As soon as he heard me say it, he rolled up next to me, calculator in hand, with a duffel bag of cash.

"Look! Look! I'm telling you, man, if you are exchanging money for this girl I will give you a better rate than the bank! Trust me. I do good business!"

"Hey, do you know what this guy is talking about?" I asked the teller.

"Ha ha, he is telling you the truth!" said the teller.

"What do you mean?"

"He gives better rates than we can."

"Is it real money?"

"Yes!"

"Then why do you let him in the bank? Isn't this hurting your business?"

The teller covered her mouth and laughed, then gathered herself and answered my question.

"We don't 'let' him. We try to get him out every day, but he always comes back. He's just trying to make a living. And he gives better rates. Why should we care?"

For a second, I felt like I was an agent for The Man, but I had to point something out.

"Because you work for the bank!"

"Who cares about the bank! The bank rips people off," said the teller, laughing.

"I love this," said Dena.

"Do you understand what's going on?"

"I mean, I can't understand what you're saying but I can see that this dude is trying to exchange my money and those girls are laughing but don't care. Does this guy just undercut the bank every day?"

"Yeah! They said that they try to get him out, but they can't, so they just let him stay."

"That's fucking awesome," said Dena.

We exchanged our money with the dude and booked it to the bus station. I was bracing myself for the worst bus ride of all time, figuring that if Chinatown buses in America were bad, the O.G. actual China buses would be exponentially shittier, but they weren't. The bus station was crowded and loud and full of people with panda hats taking buses to meet real pandas, but it was just nice enough that Port Authority hung on to its title as the undisputed worst place on Earth.

On a wall of the bus station, there was a picture map of the Sichuan bus routes with photos and arrows pointing to Emei Shan, the Giant Buddha in Leshan, and the Panda Reservation, among other things, which made it really easy to navigate our way toward Puxian's mountain.

About twenty minutes into the ride, I got hungry, since I hadn't eaten breakfast, so I broke out a Quest Bar that Emery had given me. He figured that if I was having stomach problems, I should stick to things that were easy to break down, like protein bars. I got cookies and cream flavor because once a chef, always a chef, and even protein bars should come in late-'80s, artisanal, suburban mini-mall flavors. I opened the wrapper, took a bite, and within five minutes, it happened.

"Fuck me."

"What?" asked Dena.

"I think that was a wet one," I said sheepishly.

"Oh, boo. Did you just poop your pants?"

"No. Just a little bit."

"I mean, if I was you, I'd say something like 'Dena . . . there's no such thing as pooping your pants a little bit. It's like sucking a dick. Either there's a penis in your mouth or there's poop on your pants, so did you poop your pants?' But I'm not you, so I'm going to be my nice self and let you think that you pooped your pants just a little bit."

"Oh my god, I hate you."

"A lot or a little bit?" she said, laughing.

I was hurting so bad that I had to squeeze my glutes and sit up to force the gas back up into my stomach like some sort of tai chi ass master. I've never had to shit so bad in my life, so I looked at the wrapper to try and figure out what just happened. I hadn't eaten anything all day, so it shouldn't have been this bad.

I turned the wrapper of my Quest Bar over and realized that it had eighteen grams of fiber, which normally I would appreciate, but not today. The fiber entering my belly full of hot pot BenGay combined to create a Chinese New Year fireworks extravaganza.

"Should I ask the bus driver to stop?"

"NO! We have to get to Emei Shan. I'll make it to the rest stop."

"Are you sure?"

"POSITIVE. I GOT THIS," I said with every muscle in my face clenched.

But I didn't got this. I didn't got this at all. When we pulled into the rest area, the bus wasn't even at a full stop by the time I was halfway down the aisle elbowing anyone who tried to get up and get off the bus before me. I booked it to the bathroom running with my legs together tightening my ass and holding up my pants. Once I got to the bathroom, I just went for the first open stall, bracing myself again for the terrors of municipal Chengdu.

Despite being totally prepared to sit on a piss-frosted toilet seat, the gods relented and offered me a pristine throne with toilet paper and the delightful smell of mothballs. I was in diarrhea heaven.

I plopped my ass down and unleashed a string of duck intestine hot pot feces that would have disgusted the creators of *The Human Centipede*. Angry at myself and without a shower, I thought about what Dena would say and begrudgingly wiped my ass sitting down when I heard a loud honking sound.

HAAAAAAAANNNNNNHHHHHHH!

Not sure what it was, I took my time wiping my ass and relaxed for a minute when I heard it again.

HAAAAAAAAANNNNNNNNHHHHHH!

I looked down at my phone and realized I'd gotten three texts from Dena.

Hurry up! The bus is leaving you!

Are you OK? That's the bus honking!

They're leaving! Should I get off?

Quickly, I threw on my drawers, pulled up my pants, and ran out of the bathroom, back out toward the parking lot where the bus was pulling away and Dena was walking toward the door. I chased the bus a few feet just as it was about to turn back on the highway and finally the bus driver opened the door after Dena frantically waved her arms like an inflatable air dancer.

"What the heck, man? You made the whole bus wait twenty minutes! What the hell were you doing in there?" said the bus driver.

"I'm sorry, I'm sorry! I ate hot pot last night and have diarrhea," I said, bowing my head in shame.

"Half this bus ate hot pot last night, but you're the only one with diarrhea! Maybe you should stop eating hot pot," said the bus driver.

"OK, OK, sorry."

We walked back to our seats.

"I didn't know what to say. He couldn't understand me, but I kept waving my arms at him to stop."

"Thanks, I just had to rest for a second after taking that shit. I couldn't move."

"It's cool . . . just DON'T eat again."

Once we got out of Chengdu City, it was the China you've seen in every Maoist propaganda poster since the Revolution. Dark-skinned Chinese people with homemade sandals and conical hats tending fields, leading water buffalo and chasing chickens all along the highway. This region is where my father's family is from, one province over in Hunan.

Every time I'd been back to China or Taiwan, I saw these scenes and got emotional, thinking that that could have been my life if my grandparents hadn't fled to Taiwan. I saw people trying to sell boiled peanuts along the side of the road, just like my grandpa would. For overseas Chinese kids going home, riding these roads can feel like watching your ancestors under the big top, like the circus animals that never got free.

"This is beautiful," she said.

"It is. It's beautiful until it's you working that paddy."

"I know. . . . Why do you have to ruin everything, panda?"

"I'm not. I'm just being realistic. I don't want to indulge myself in ruin porn."

"It's not ruined, though. I get it, no one wants to wake up and go work a rice paddy, but it's still beautiful, what they are doing."

"Yeah, but the people that glorify and romanticize this are trying to get these people to keep doing it. It's cultural coercion."

"I just want to pay respect to it and honor it because somebody has to do it."

"But that sentiment is to justify our roles. It's for us to feel pain and derive pleasure from that pain and tell ourselves that somebody has to do this. It's us 'remembering,' but they don't have to 'remember' 'cause they live this like *Groundhog Day*."

"Well, what are you going to do about it?"

"I think we have to pay them more."

She always seemed to ask me the right questions. We're always told to pay homage to the farmers. Pay homage to the workers. Lay our treasures up to whatever country we're in, but when are we going to actually pay the farmers and workers?*

---

* This is my girl Elena Bergeron's line. Not mine. She let me hold it.

———

I enjoyed talking to Dena about these things.

She was one of the few people I talked to who wouldn't blink when I mentioned the Matrix—and would then agree that there is actually a global mechanism that perpetuates the dominance of the few over the many.

She saw the strings at the puppet show, and it was this ability more than anything that made me feel like we were part of something more important than race or country or city. She was always ready to reconsider everything she'd been told, without any fear of having to erase everything she knew. Even before she met me, the world was melting before her eyes.

Her perception of Scranton, her family, her career, and music all devolved into a puddle of processed Cheez Whiz. For too long Mr. Fusco had shielded her by draping her in dominant culture. But when he finally set her free, the visions were paralyzing.

Dena wanted to act, but everything that sounded like a good idea Monday, she'd talk herself out of by Wednesday. Whether it was singing or cooking or designing, she was looking for one action or one work or one profession that could contain her entire purpose, do it, and be done. Eager to give herself to this purpose, it eluded her. Whatever she wanted to do with her life, she was probably already doing. She just had to keep going.

Thoughts about Dena rushed through my head as the landscape unscrolled around us. I'd never been happier with anyone in my life, and as our lives continued to change, Dena clung tight; she made me her everything. It was surreal that another human voluntarily attached herself to me, but I also needed her to love herself. By proposing, I felt like I could put her fears to rest: I'm committed. I'm here for you, but it's time for you to be here for yourself.

I suddenly thought about proposing to her right there on the bus. But I wasn't about to appropriate a poverty landscape as the backdrop for my own romance. Still: I felt one with her at that moment because she was seeing the motherland.

I don't believe in country.

I don't believe in race.

But I do believe in the power of place.

Our spirits have a connection to place that is undeniable. When I arrive in New York on the red-eye and spill off the Manhattan Bridge in a yellow cab, I get chills. When the door to my parents' home opens and I smell the scent of my family, it reconnects me. And when I cruise rural southwestern China—the land of my ancestors—it settles me.

Until Dena came to see this land, too, I felt like I had hidden something from her. I'd seen her family in Scranton; I'd had the Seven Fishes Dinner, Thanksgiving, and Easter. But my roots were something she had to see and love before we would be for real.

I watched her look out the window soaking in everything about the ride and appreciating it.

"I gotta learn Chinese," she said.

"You ain't lie."

We got to the Leshan bus stop and walked up the mountain to the hot springs. Fish was going to show us around since it was his hometown, but he had to take care of some things first. While we waited, we waded around in hot springs flavored with honeydew, chocolate, passion fruit, and Chinese herbs. There was red water, purple water, and even an exfoliating hot spring where little minnows nibbled at your dead skin. Never doubt China's ability to make something organic and natural like hot springs super fucking weird.

After an hour or so, our skin started to prune, so we walked around. Toward the back of the hot springs was a lounging area where Dena saw the first white people she'd seen since landing in Chengdu the day before.

"It's only been one day but it's kind of weird to see white people again."

"I know. I mean, not just 'cause you're white, but it felt weird to see you at the airport yesterday."

"I know, panda! It scared me. But it's natural. And we always sink right back in."

"It's bugged out, though. I think about you every day, but I just felt disconnected when I saw you."

"Do you still feel that way?"

"No. We good, ma." I kissed her.

We looked at these two big-boned European women speaking what seemed to be Dutch as they lay on cots by the herbal salt pool. Everything seemed normal until one of the women started to tilt her pelvis back and forth at a medium pace a few inches off the cot. Her entire body lay stiff except her buttocks and pelvis poppin' sporadically like a subwoofer.

"Oh my god. . . ."

"What?"

"That woman is doing her Kegel exercises by the herbal salt pool."

"That is so ill."

"Stop looking!"

"How can I stop? There's a middle-aged Dutch lady working her vag out by the herbal salt pool. This is some unicorn shit."

"White people are so weird," she said.

Eventually, the excitement of watching this old woman do Kegel exercises wore off. We went back to the showers, changed, and waited for Fish to arrive. Of course, Fish showed up with food in hand.

"Eddie! Dena! I want you to try. Leshan famous smoked duck!"

"Word. I love duck."

"Me, too! I've never had it smoked."

"This one not just smoked but also braised in *lu wei,* so will be familiar to Eddie," said Fish, who never forgot my Taiwanese palate.

Over the next few hours, Fish showed us restaurants like Open Smile, known for its chili-braised peel 'n' eat local shrimp, glutinous-rice-stuffed dates, and dry-wok-tossed river fish. He took us to a bar his friend owned, then drove us toward Emei Shan.

"Eddie, I know you are going to bring Dena here tomorrow, but it is very cool at night, too. We can walk around and check it out. You will not have enough time to see all of it tomorrow anyway."

"OK, cool."

We walked around the entrance to Emei Shan, where there was a relief sculpture of Puxian.

"Dena, this is Puxian. He is Buddha's eldest son!" said Fish.

"Buddha had kids?"

"Yes! This is the oldest, and Emei Shan is under his protection."

"What does he do?"

"Eddie, I will tell you in Chinese, but please tell Dena for me, OK?" said Fish. "Puxian's role is to help all of us reach enlightenment. He doesn't do it for you, but he brings out the best in all of us and gives us the help we need to be the best versions of ourselves. He also teaches us that to reach enlightenment we need to put others and the world before ourselves before we can save ourselves."

I told Dena what Fish said.

"That's really cool," she said.

I didn't think it fully registered with Dena. It felt like she was just humoring me with all this Chinese mumbo jumbo, so I spoke to Fish.

"Fish. . . . Do you believe all this stuff? Puxian and Emei Shan and how he looks after us?"

"Hmmm, this is a personal question. I am not sure, Eddie, but I respect Puxian. I revere Emei Shan. But if you ask me if I 'believe' it, I am not sure. This is a tough thing for me to answer."

"What about being 'Chinese'? Do you believe in being 'Chinese'? Is it even a thing to be 'Chinese'?"

"Eddie, this REALLY confuses me. I don't understand what you are asking me."

"What I'm saying is this. I don't think there is such a thing as 'race.' Like, people made it up. But, I *like* being Chinese, you know? If you weren't Chinese, do you think it would matter?"

"I am Chinese. I don't know anything else, Eddie. But what's wrong? Why are you asking me these questions?"

"Because, Fish, I'm not sure. I'm just not sure. What if Dena and I get married and we have kids and they don't want to be Chinese? What if she doesn't want to be Chinese? Then what do I do? Do I just let my kids grow up to speak English and eat McRibs? I'd still love them, but it'd just be sad if they didn't want to be Chinese."

"I don't know this McRib, but Eddie, you are born in America. I'm sure your parents worried, too, that going to America you may not want to be Chinese, but look at you! You found an American girl you love, you bring her back to China, you show her your homeland and you do your best to teach her the things you know. You want to be Chinese, right?"

"Yes! Of course. Even though I think a lot of things about race are bullshit, it means a lot to me. The language, the food, the way we do things, it reflects five thousand years of existence! It's not everything, because we still have to write our story, but I don't want kids with orange hair wearing shoes inside!"

"Eddie, calm down. Big deal, orange hair, right?"

"No, you're right, I'm just being funny. I don't care if they have orange hair or like orange chicken, but I don't want them to be cut off from our history. I don't want them to forget our beginning."

"Ahhh, Eddie. They will know. If you love it this much, I'm sure they will, too. Let me ask you, why do you like being Chinese so much?"

It wasn't that I *liked* it, exactly.

"It's not just that I like it. I owe it, Fish. It gave too much for me to ever deny it."

This is my face.

This is my place.

This is my beginning.

I am Taiwanese. I am Chinese. I am American. This history isn't mine to control. It's mine to give.

Fish spoke. "Eddie, for someone like me to meet *huaren** like you, it is special to see you come home and appreciate our culture. For many of us, we are not sure if you will like it. You have a face like ours, but we are

---

*   Overseas Chinese.

different, you and me. Very different, and we get worried, too, that you will not understand us or look down on us because America is big brother."

"Fish, I'm little brother over there, too. . . . Don't forget it."

He marinated on it for a second, but I wasn't finished.

"I have to ask you one more question, Fish. What do you think makes us Chinese?"

"I can answer this for you, Xiao Ming! There is an old saying: 'Li yi zhi bang.' A country based on manners, values, and way of treating people. We are proud of our manners. We are proud of our values. That is China!"

I was right all along! It was about taking your shoes off inside, pouring tea for your elders, paying respect to your grandparents, and asking if you've eaten upon meeting. Not just those specific mannerisms and actions, but the underlying intention. The idea that these things represent a feeling, a connection, a humanity . . . a way to love.

But then another thought popped into my head. OK, many thoughts popped into my head: the drivers screaming down six-lane roads in the rain with no regard for the people pushing rickshaws through the road with makeshift sandals on, the guy who drove the moped through the hallway at Hakka Homes, the bus driver who almost left me with skid marks in my drawers in the bathroom. Was this the Chinese way?

"Fish, let me ask you, though. . . . Do you think China is behaving well?"

"No way! Man, us real Chinese have forgotten who we are. Everything is developing too fast, and we have lost our way. To be honest, we're gonna have to depend on you Chinese people. . . ."

"What Chinese people?"

"You and Dena Chinese people, that's who! You are Chinese! So will Dena! Don't forget it."

I had lost track of Dena.

"Dena! Where'd you go?"

"Hey! I'm over here," she cried out from next to a waterfall.

"My bad. I was talking to Fish. What have you been doing?"

"This mountain is awesome. I took photos of all the art, the signs, and information so that I can send it to my mom. I think she'd really like it."

She broke out her phone and flipped through all the photos, perfectly taken, perfectly framed, some with filters and others brightened.

"If Dena like this, we can go to back side! There is a temple you can see at night."

We got back in the car, drove to the temple right in front of two giant double red doors. Dena got out of the car and started walking toward the entrance, and it hit me.

"Fish. . . . Unlock your trunk."

"Why? What happened?"

"I need to get the ring, and it is in the trunk."

"Oh! Oh god! Right now? Right now? We do this right now?"

"Yeah, let's go to the car but act normal."

"OK, OK, I act normal. How do I act normal? Eddie! You are supposed to do this tomorrow, when I'm not around. How do I act normal? You tell me how to act normal!"

"What is Fish freaking out about?" asked Dena from twenty feet away.

"Nothing. Nothing, we just gotta get something in the trunk."

"Fish. . . . Calm down, man. Just open the trunk."

"OK! OK! Trunk . . . trunk . . . trunk, open! Open!"

I found my backpack, looked down at my Jumpman slides, tugged at the Redskins jersey on my chest, and thought to myself.

It was meant to be. Chanclas, Redskins, my mother's ring, these are a few of my favorite things. I took a deep breath, turned toward Dena, black box in hand, and walked over. My heart was jumpin' out the gym, my legs felt like *ai yu* jelly, and everything in my body told me to turn around, but I didn't.

I told every fearful, ignorant, insecure bone in my body to shut the fuck up and ride or die with me.

It was time.

Halfway to Dena, about eight feet away, she turned. There was horror on her face. She saw the box in my hand, but I didn't stop. I just kept on moving, found my spot about a foot in front of her and assumed the position on one knee.

"Dena, I love you. I love you more than I ever thought I could love someone, and although I'm scared, although I'm nervous, I'm figuring out in this moment how to love . . . so bear with me.

"You've been ready for me, and you're everything I've ever wanted in a best friend, and I just didn't know. I didn't know because I didn't like myself. There were things I wanted to change, and there were things I was afraid you'd see, but until I peeled it all back and let you see, I couldn't know. I couldn't know that you really loved ME.

"The shitty me.

"The stupid me.

"The Chinese me.

"The worst fiber-eating diarrhea-on-the-bus parts of me, but you do. You love me, and I never, ever thought anyone but my mom could love me, but you do. And. . . ."

"Eddie, shut up! Just shut up! You're making no sense!"

"What?"

"Just ask me, dummy! Just ask me!"

"What? Will you marry me?"

"YES!"

"Yes, like, Ask you to marry me, or yes, like, You'll marry me?"

"YES! I WILL MARRY YOU! YES! Oh my god, you were just talking nonsense forever, and I couldn't understand anything and my heart was racing and I was just like 'I have to let him finish, but he is making no sense right now!' I'm sorry I cut you off, boo, but I had to. You aren't making any sense today. . . ."

I picked her up. I might have grabbed some ass. And I kissed her.

"I know. I've been a mess waiting for you."

She rubbed her nose against mine, put her arms over my shoulders and scrunched her face.

"It's OK, Panda. . . . I'm here."

———

The next day, we woke up in Leshan.

I was clear-eyed and happy. . . . But there was trepidation to my vibe.

Something had changed. It was good change, it was a change we both wanted, but still it was change and I don't think either of us had fully processed what happened, or what was still happening. Luckily, we were alone, just Dena and I, all brand-new walking down Leshan to find breakfast.

Neither of us could sleep in. We were excited to be together.

Everything Hakka Heather told me about the heavens beaming down directly to Sichuan rang true. The world looked different. It was as if Moses parted the smog for one day and we could see all the way back to the beginning of time. Before the institution of marriage, before the right to procreate, it was just Original Man and Original Boo walking down a mountain looking for breakfast.

That day, the universe allowed me to pull back the curtain on the past and touch what I believe everything in life is about: how we love.

Dena and I held hands, we soaked up the sun, but we didn't talk much. Everything had already been said. Looking down Leshan, I realized that I'd lived my last day as an autonomous sovereign state. From this day forward, we were a union: both parts of the whole.

Every store on the road down Leshan was once a garage or still a garage but also a store. Above the garages were homes. Together, they were a neighborhood. Some stores sold spare parts, others outdated electronics, but most still had their gates down. Dena and I were so eager to see the rest of our lives, we didn't realize it was 8 A.M. We took a right turn at the foot of the mountain and saw people shuffling around. Gates went up, rice cookers started giving off steam, and everyone began presenting their wares. About twenty minutes later, we settled on the first food stall that was open: just a woman, her daughter, pig's feet, spicy cow intestines, pork belly, and meatballs.

"What do you think?" I asked Dena.

"Looks good." She smiled.

We sat down on folding stools and ordered one of each. It arrived immediately at exactly 140 degrees.*

I looked at Dena, I ate the food, and I finally let it happen. I was accepted.

The movie should have ended there. Second-generation Taiwanese-Chinese-American man meets third-generation Italian-Irish American in N.Y., falls in love, brings her back on the mothership, asks her to marry him, and they consummate the decision over pig's feet and spicy cow intestines. Mayor De Blasio rises from his seat in the Ziegfeld Theatre at the premiere declaring that multiculturalism and affordable housing are alive and well in N.Y. President Xi Jinping watches it simultaneously in Chengdu and forgives Marco Polo for all his transgressions, states that Dena Fusco is more beautiful than Julia Roberts ever was, and exclaims that this movie shits all over *Eat, Pray, Love*. He immediately announces plans for a bootleg Tibetan version of our story called *Eat, Fuck, Yak Meatballs* that promotes the Chinese Dream. At least that's what should have happened.

Eighteen months later, we broke up.

But I remember Leshan. That day love obliterated me. Everything I knew about life and family were shattered and replaced. I embraced it all. We were love, we were family, we might have even been Chinese. All that time, my fears—about identity and family and love— were misplaced. It isn't acceptance that extinguishes us, instead, it awakens us. And even if the love doesn't last, acceptance gives us new beginnings.

---

* I know, because I use a similar steam table to hold food at Baohaus.

———

A few days later, we rode to the airport together. She lay on my lap tired from the trip. Luckily, she didn't miss anything. There were no idyllic images of farmers in the paddies or kids chasing free-range chickens. No visions of strong communist women with wheat thrown over their shoulders, just good old government housing, power lines, and construction everywhere you looked.

I took a break from the world outside my window and looked at this cab driver's medallion. According to the official license, he'd been driving for what seemed like twenty-some years. In the photo was the face of what looked like a young Stephen Chow on the up and up, pre–*Kung Fu Hustle*. Curious if it was him, I had to ask.

"Sifu! How long have you been driving?"

"Just like the paper says! I started August eighth, 1998."

"That's a lucky day! Good fortune with all those eights."

"Yeah, right! I'm so tired of driving. Those cot damn eights brought me fifteen long years of driving. But the longer I drive, the lazier I get. I used to drive twenty-four-hour days three to four days a week, now only sixteen hours four days a week, but still. . . . All I do is drive."

I think to myself that even sixteen-hour shifts for fifteen years sounds insane.

"Sixteen? Am I hearing you right, sixteen?"

"Yes! Sixteen. Some of my friends drive twenty-four still and take every other day off, but then you're guaranteed to get sick. They all have illnesses, but we still try to drive as much as we can every day, 'cause no matter what, you have to pay three hundred fifty RMB to the boss. We make sixty to seventy RMB an hour with a break for lunch and a break for dinner."

I did the math in my head quickly, 65 times 14 minus 350 equaled 560. Then 560 multiplied by the exchange rate I pulled up on Google equaled . . .

"*Wa sai!* You only make ninety U.S. dollars every day."

"You're telling me. Tough shit out here."

I look back at his photo from 1998. I was starting eleventh grade when this dude started driving twenty-four-hour days making probably less than $90 a day. I think about what I wanted to be when I was seventeen and then what he wanted for himself in 1998. He was smiling in his photo, not a cheesy smile, but g'd up like Stephen Chow ice grill'd. I wonder if he has kids.

"Sifu, sorry to pry, but do you have kids?"

"No problem. I like talking to you. Sometimes you go hours without talking to anyone in these cars. It gets depressing, man, but yeah, I got a kid. Fifteen years old. Testing for high school this year."

"How's he doing?"

"He is a smart kid, but he just keeps playing damn video games! I tell him that testing for high school is the most important thing for his life right now, but he doesn't listen or care about anything. He's just addicted to these damn video games."

He sounded like my mother, and I smiled. I thought about how much I used to love video games. I used to play a lot more. Come to think of it, I used to watch a lot more Knicks games, too. Why hadn't I even opened my Xbox after we moved? Why was I missing NBA summer league in fucking China?

Half asleep, Dena adjusted herself on my lap, waking me from this naive daydream. She wiped her nose with the back of her palm, tilted her head and stretched out her back before settling onto my lap. I waited a beat to make sure she was asleep and then tapped the glass to get the cab driver's attention.

"Sifu, just wait till he finds a girl."

Acknowledgments

Ellen.
Emery.
Evan.
Mom & Dad.
Chris Jackson.
Rafael & Christina.
Elena.
Marc.
Amir.
Julie & Cindy.
Steve.
Joe.
CV the god.
Adrian.
Dan & Jen.
Shane & Tamyka.
Daniel.
Ray & Jill.
Bernard & Amy.
Jim.
Mel.
Rocky Li.
Rabbi.

Fish.

Hakka Ellen.

Xiao Zhen.

Tim.

Prodigy.

Marvis.

Berto.

Leon.

Sparkz.

Stephane.

Jay.

Roseanna & Jarrett.

Brian & Jess.

Sena & Mike.

April. Nico. China.

Paul.

Rocky.

Kenzo.

Warren.

Romaen.

Nick.

It's been a tough year. Thanks for being there for me.

What's understood doesn't need to be said.

e

EDDIE HUANG is the world's first and only Human Panda. He splits time between Brooklyn and Malibu, playing basketball and boogie boarding. Cam'ron is his favorite rapper, soup dumplings are his favorite food, and Kristaps Porzingis is his favorite basketball player. This year he listened to a lot of Future. He also likes the Washington Redskins but thinks they should change their name. His online dating profile reads "Single Asiatic male seeks ride or die chick."

Facebook.com/mreddiehuang

@MrEddieHuang

ABOUT THE TYPE

This book was set in Electra, a typeface designed for Linotype by renowned type designer W. A. Dwiggins (1880–1956). Electra is a fluid typeface, avoiding the contrasts of thick and thin strokes that are prevalent in most modern typefaces.